Twenty-five New Walks in and around Hertfordshire

To Ann
my companion on all these walks and elsewhere

Twenty-five New Walks in and around Hertfordshire

John A. Vaughan

These walks have been researched and prepared for the
St Michael's Ramblers of Birchwood, Hatfield, Herts

Ellingham Press

ISBN 978-0-9926031-8-2

Printed and bound by Graphics and Print, Telford

Ellingham Press, 43 High Street, Much Wenlock, Shropshire TF13 6AD

www.ellinghampress.co.uk

Introduction

All of the routes included in this book are original and have not been published elsewhere. They were devised, researched and led by Ann and John Vaughan for the St. Michael's Ramblers of Hatfield. However in the nature of such things, some sections of these routes will have been used by other planners. Remember that the mere existence of a footpath indicates that others have already walked it. A shorter version of each walk is also included wherever possible.

The routes described were all correct at the time of publication. They are suitable for obedient dogs unless otherwise specified; however dogs may have to be kept on a lead in some sections. Starting points are located in free parking areas, but some car parks may have instituted a charge since the routes were checked.

The St. Michael's Ramblers were founded after an Easter Pilgrimage to St. Alban's Abbey produced requests from the pilgrims for more frequent group walks. After more than ten years, they have now completed well over a hundred rambles. The Ramblers are enormously indebted to their couriers Jill, Pauline and Rosemary, who take the lunch orders so that by the time the lunch stop is reached, the food is almost on the table.

John A. Vaughan

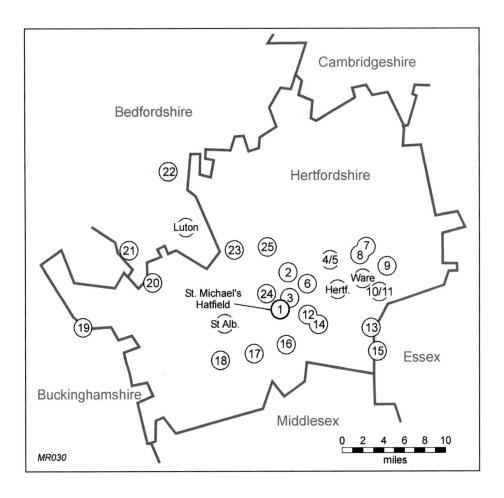

Cambridgeshire

Bedfordshire

Hertfordshire

㉒

Luton

㉑ ㉓ ㉕ ⑦ ⑧ ⑨

⑳ ② ④/5
⑥ Ware
Hertf. 10/11

St. Michael's
Hatfield ㉔ ③
① ⑫
St Alb. ⑭ ⑬

⑲ ⑯ ⑮ Essex

⑱ ⑰

Buckinghamshire

Middlesex

MR030

0 2 4 6 8 10
miles

6

1: Hatfield – Birchwood to Lemsford

This walk starts and finishes at St. Michael and All Angels Church in Birchwood, Hatfield. Conceived as a winter walk that would require no driving from the meeting point by the church, the route uses parts of the Lea Valley Walk.

OS Explorer 182, Land Ranger 166,
Distance: 7 miles (11.2 km),
Time: 3¾ hours,
A shorter 4.8 mile (7.7 km) version is also shown,
Park: Car park beside St. Michael's Church on Birchwood Avenue

AL10 0QW, GR TL226095,
Route: Footpaths, bridleways and pavements, some climb-over stiles, not suitable for dogs as there are several fields with livestock, also Stanborough Park can be crowded, Access: Buses No. 300 at Birchwood and 366 at Lemsford, trains at Hatfield Station. Refreshments: Public houses in Lemsford and Birchwood.

The St. Michael's Ramblers first walked a version of this route on January 7, 2006.

---

1. From the car park, turn right, then right again at the roundabout to walk up Ground Lane.
2. After 200 yd, turn right along the Alban Way that follows the route of the former Hatfield to St. Albans railway.
3. At the first footbridge, leave the Alban Way to the right, and then turn right along the pavement of Wellfield Road.
4. Just before the roundabout, turn right along the service road. At the end, cross Birchwood Avenue and turn left to follow the pavement for 100 yd along West View to a light-controlled pedestrian crossing over the A414.
5. Use the lights to cross the road and continue across the footbridge over the A1(M) motorway. Go straight on to cross Green Lanes, then turn right and follow the pavement 400 yd to where Astwick Avenue emerges from the left.
6. Cross Green Lanes to enter a wide track opposite with Tesco's tower visible ahead.

Follow this track for three-quarters of a mile, passing a right angle turn to the left, until the track bends left again towards a farm.

7. Cross the stile on the right, keep on the same heading and go over a narrow field to another stile. Cross this stile, go between houses and turn left along the pavement of a road to a roundabout.
8. For the shorter 4.8 mile walk, turn downhill under the A1(M), carefully cross the dual carriageway that carries heavy traffic, enter the adjacent car park, cross over the River Lea and then continue from Point 16.
For the complete walk, take care and follow the pavement clockwise round the roundabout where traffic seems to arrive at high speed from any direction. Cross both Coopers Green Lane and Brocket Road, then turn left along the pavement of Brocket Road.
9. After 300 yd, turn right into New Road and at the Great North

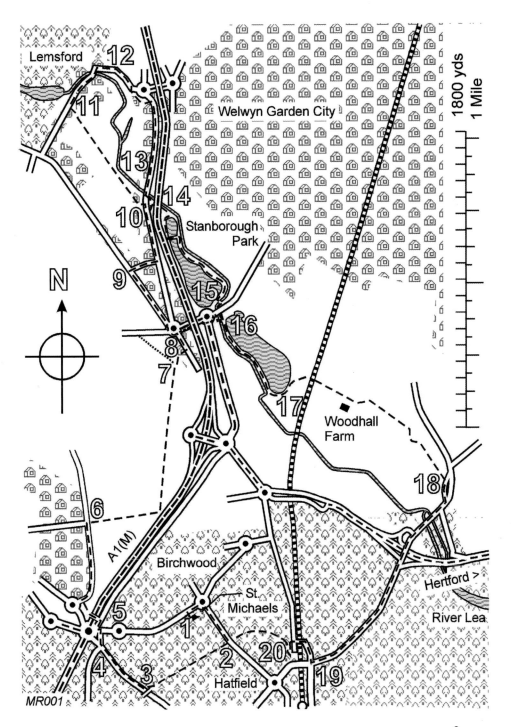

Lemsford

12

11

Welwyn Garden City

13

14

10

Stanborough
Park

N

9

15

16

8

7

17

Woodhall
Farm

18

6

A1(M)

Birchwood

St.
Michaels

Hertford >

River Lea

5

1

4

3

2

20

19

Hatfield

1800 yds
1 Mile

MR001

Road, turn left. Go along the pavement for 250 yd to a footpath on the left signed for Lemsford.

10. Follow this path which soon turns right across pasture land. Continue virtually straight on, crossing several stiles to emerge between houses in Lemsford.

11. Turn downhill, pass a watermill, headquarters of Ramblers Worldwide Holidays, and also locally reputed to be "The Old Mill on The Stream". Continue over the River Lea between public houses and cross the road just beyond the bridge and turn right towards a roundabout.

12. Just before the roundabout, re-cross the road to follow a service road up to the Great North Road, then continue along the pavement to the right.

13. After 300 yd, go over the River Lea, then a few yards further on, cross the road and enter a twisted path by the river that goes under the motorway into Stanborough Park.

14. Turn right beside the lake and cross the long footbridge. Turn right again to follow the path between river and lake for 300 yd to a bridge over the river beside Stanborough Road.

15. Cross this bridge and go under the road on a path beside the river.

16. Emerge to follow the path between sailing lake and river, continuing as the route curves round the far end of the lake.

17. Take the path that goes through an arch under the railway and carry on across fields. Go a quarter mile beyond Woodhall Farm to reach a narrow road beside Mill Green Lane.

18. Turn right on this road to join Mill Green Lane and continue along the pavement. Cross both streams of the River Lea and the Hertford Road (A414). Go on with Hatfield Park on the left and houses on the right for half a mile to traffic lights.

19. Turn right for 100 yd, then left over the footbridge crossing the railway line. Continue across the road beyond the bridge.

20. Enter a footpath signed for St. Albans and the Galleria; this is the start of the Alban Way. This path first turns sharp left, then right to follow a route that curves left again in a cutting between house gardens.
Walk a further 400 yd to reach Ground Lane and then turn right downhill to retrace the outward route from the start point.

2: Welwyn Garden City I – North Side Mostly on Footpaths

This walk starts beneath Digswell Railway Viaduct beside the Hertford Road on the north side of Welwyn Garden City. It makes a circuit of the north-east of the town, returning via more open countryside.

OS Explorer 182, Land Ranger 166,
Distance: 5.3 miles (8.5 km),
Time: 3 hours,
No shorter version is indicated,
Park: Car park almost under the viaduct on Digswell Park Road at the junction with Hertford Road – AL6 0DB, GR TL246150,

Route: Woodland paths, short sections of grass verge, pavements, and farm tracks, paths may be muddy after rain, no stiles, several notable hills.
Access: Five minute walk from buses No. 300, 301 and 388 on Bessemer Road, trains to Welwyn North,
Refreshments: Bar and restaurant on Panshanger Golf Course and at Tewin Bury.

The St. Michael's Ramblers first walked this route on November 5, 2011.

1. From the car park, turn right under the viaduct, walk along the grass verge and cross the River Mimram.
2. Where the road bears right, enter a footpath on the left. Follow this path about 100 yd to reach Bessemer Road. **This road carries busy traffic.**
3. Cross the road and enter the pathway opposite which climbs up through woods. Follow the path for about a quarter of a mile to reach St. John's Church, Digswell.
4. Follow the pavement round to the right of the church then go across the front of Digswell House to enter a straight path between trees.
5. Cross Knightsfield and continue on the same line along a green way that enters Sherrardspark Woods. Keep on along the same path for about a quarter mile as it dips left, then starts up a brisk but short climb. Go past a memorial seat on the right.
6. At the next crossing by a solitary marker post, with a "multi-route" post 100 yd further on, turn left on a path that soon has houses ahead. Pass the houses to emerge on Pently Park.
7. Turn right down Pently Park, following it 200 yd to reach Colneydale.

8. Turn left into Colneydale and follow it 200 yd down to Digswell Road.
9. Cross Digswell Road near a double roundabout and go almost straight ahead along Digswell Rise. Continue over the railway and turn left immediately.
10. At Knightsfield, turn right and follow the pavement to Bessemer Road (A1000) by a roundabout. Turn right along Bessemer Road and continue to the underpass by the next roundabout at Mundells.
11. Go through the underpass, then follow the pavement downhill. Bear left away from the road to walk with grass on the right and houses on the left to a path leading to an underpass on the right. Continue straight on across the grass and cross the B1000 (Waterside) to the car park opposite. Turn left down a grassy path, then turn right along a paved footpath to a lake.
12. Turn along the right side of the lake, continuing under a bridge beneath Herns Way.
13. Turn left up to the pavement beside the road and continue uphill to the roundabout.
14. At the roundabout, cross left and walk along Herns Lane. Then turn left again to go down to the end of Old Herns Lane. Go through a gap in the hedge and emerge on the Hertford Road.

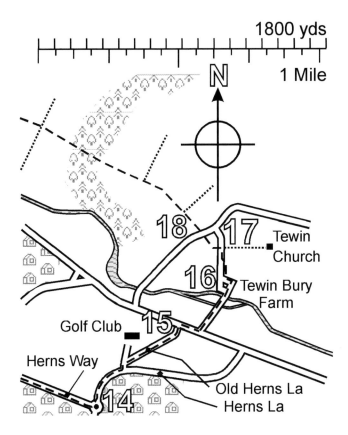

This road carries really fast-moving traffic.

15. Cross the road and turn right along the grass verge to the entry for Tewin Bury Farm. Turn left into the approach to the farm and cross bridges over two branches of the River Mimram.

   Go past a sign directing traffic to the left and continue to a yellow reception building.

16. Turn left along the exit road - **with traffic coming towards you.**

   At a junction of several roads, turn right up a gravel track, and then go 200 yd along a metalled road.

17. Where a footpath crosses the track and Tewin church can be seen to the right, turn left on a path through woods.

18. After 150 yd, cross a lane and enter a wide track opposite, with a concrete strip and hedge on the left. Continue across open fields and through a band of woodland. After about a mile, the track changes to a footpath.

   Follow it downhill, still beside the concrete strip, for a further three-quarters of a mile to emerge on New Road.

19. Turn left downhill to the roundabout on the Hertford Road. Then turn right, towards the viaduct and after 100 yd cross the road back to the start point.

3: Welwyn Garden City II – East Side Mostly on Footpaths

Starting from the King George V Playing Field in Welwyn Garden City, this walk makes a circuit of the east side of the town. It was intended as a bracing after-Christmas walk that could be completed without a break while offering unusual glimpses of a familiar town.

OS Explorer 182, Land Ranger 166,
Distance: 6 miles (9.7 km),
Time: 3¼ hours,
A shorter 3.2 mile (5.1 km) version is also shown,
Park: King George V Playing Field

off Beehive Lane in the south east of the town – AL7 48W, GR TL251113
Route: Greenways, back alleys, footpaths, pavements, and a grass verge, paths may be muddy after rain, there is one steep hill and one easy climb-over stile,
Access: Buses No. 301, 330, 366, 403

Refreshments: Public house a few yards from the entrance to the Playing Field car park.

The St. Michael's Ramblers first walked this route on January 2, 2010.

1. Start down the concrete path that runs from the car park beside the bowling green and turn right at the T-junction. Go straight across a road and keep left in the green way as it curves right.
2. Cross diagonally right over a second road, and keep on along a green way, stay left of central bushes as the way curves right. Cross Thumbswood, keeping the same line across the corner of a grass triangle and over Moorlands. Take the path beside the hedge on the right of the green way and go through a wooded section to emerge beside Howlands House.
3. **Take care: the road here carries heavy traffic.** Cross the road and enter The Commons Nature Reserve, by the path on the left side. Follow this path for 200 yd and go through a gate to continue along a wide area with trees on either side. After 400 yd, the path leads to a wide gate.
4. Take the narrow path to the right of the gate along the edge of a field and eventually cross a footbridge. Turn left just beyond the bridge and follow a grass path between a small stream and a fence.
5. After 300 yd where the main path turns left out of the reserve, take a path to the right and meet the first of several sections of duckboard. Continue past a pond and information board and take the left path at a Y-junction to emerge through a metal gate on to a wide green way.
6. Keep on the same line through the centre of the green way for 300 yd. Cross a road and go another 250 yd to Cole Green Lane.
7. **Take care: this road carries heavy traffic.** Cross the road, turn right and follow the pavement, turning left at the junction with Black Fan Road. Go past one roundabout to a second one by a supermarket, then turn right to cross Black Fan Road for Panshanger Drive.
8. For the shorter 3.2 mile walk, stay on the right-hand side of the road

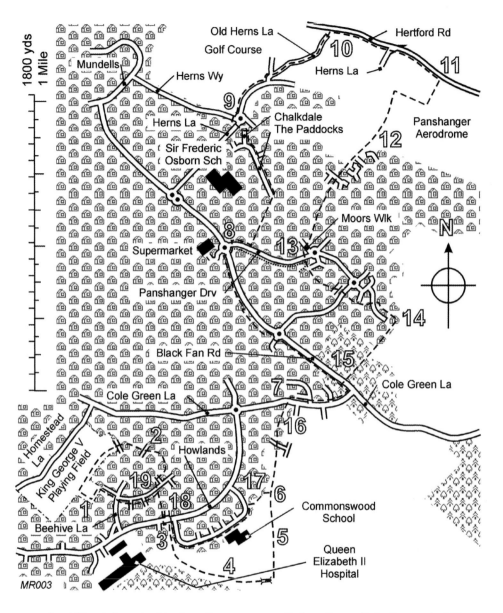

for 400 yd, then just before the roundabout with Moors Walk, turn right into the marked footpath and continue from Point 13.

For the complete walk, cross Panshanger Drive and follow the left side for 150 yd, then turn left on a path beside a playing field.

Follow the path to the end of The Paddocks, continuing along the pavement to turn right into Chalkdale.

9. At the far end of Chalkdale, climb steps to the roundabout and walk round it clockwise, crossing both Herns Lane and Herns Way.

Continue along a further section of Herns Way and turn left into the approach to Panshanger Golf Club. Immediately, cross the approach and walk right down Old Herns Lane.

10. At the end of the lane, go through a gap on to the grass verge of the Hertford Road. **Take care: this road carries fast-moving traffic.** Stay on the nearer verge as the far one gets too narrow for safety. Turn right and walk beside the road on the right-hand verge. Cross a junction (Herns Lane) and continue on the verge for 400 yd to a gap in the hedge on the right.

11. Go through the gap and up a footpath that climbs steeply between a fence and a hedge. At the top, the path turns sharply to the right, then left across the end of Panshanger Aerodrome.

12. Keep straight ahead on pretty much the same line, as the path skirts the ends of several residential roads, then crosses one and runs behind a row of houses, to emerge 400 yd further on near a roundabout.

13. Go anticlockwise to cross Moors Walk and Panshanger Drive then enter a marked path opposite and take the left-hand branch past back gardens. Continue along this path as it curves left for 300 yd and crosses two roads close together.

Skirt the end of a third road, cross a fourth to a path with the backs of houses on the right and allotments on the left and go on to a T-junction.

14. Turn right along a track through a wood that ends on Black Fan Road.

15. **Take care: this road carries heavy traffic.** Cross the road, turn left along the pavement, then turn right into Cole Green Lane and continue along the pavement until opposite the green way walked earlier at Point 7.

16. Walk back along the green way until the metal gate is reached at the end of the grassy area.

17. Keep right, walking between trees on the left and houses on the right. Eventually go past a diagonal block of garages on the right to emerge on a road.
Turn left to follow the pavement past Commonswood school and continue as the road curves left to Howlands.

18. **Take care: this road carries heavy traffic.** Cross the road and go back along the path beside Howlands House almost opposite.

19. At the far end, turn left along the pavement to Beehive Lane. Cross the lane and enter the approach to the car park to return to the start point.

4:   Stapleford I – North to Watton-at-Stone

This walk starts at Stapleford, a few miles north of Hertford on the A119, and crosses high land on its way to Watton-at-Stone. It returns along the course of the River Beane footpath, part of the Hertfordshire Way.

OS Explorer 194, Land Ranger 166,
Distance: 6 miles (9.7 km),
Time: 3¼ hours,
A 3.5 mile (5.6 km) version is also shown,
Park: In service road beside A119 a quarter mile north of the railway bridge at Stapleford –

SG14 3NW, GR TL309169,
Route: Footpaths, bridleways and quiet lanes, paths may be muddy after rain, several stiles including two high ladder stiles over walls, so neither route is suitable for dogs,
Access: Buses No. 390 at Stapleford, 383, 390 and 203 at Watton-at-Stone, Hertford Loop trains to Watton,
Refreshments: Public houses in Stapleford and Watton-at-Stone.

The St. Michael's Ramblers first walked this route on April 5, 2008.

---

1. From the start point, turn right into Church Lane to walk eastwards along a part of the Hertfordshire Way. Cross a narrow stream, then after 200 yd, cross the principal stream of the River Beane. Continue along the lane past Stapleford church and school then start to climb between hedges.
2. Just beyond a sharp turn to the right, go through a gate stile on the left. Remember first to look back over the village and note that you have already climbed higher than the church spire. Follow the well-defined footpath for about a quarter mile across rough ground towards a clearly visible gate stile. This leads to a farm track.
3. Turn left along the track towards Southend Farm. After 100 yd, turn right by a footpath marker to go over a small bridge and through the hedge into a field.
    Turn left towards a stile and climb over it. Then follow the path through a small wood to emerge in an open field.
4. Turn right and walk along the edge of the field to a road.
5. Turn left along this road; there may be some traffic, but the low banks on either side should allow approaching vehicles to be seen in good time.

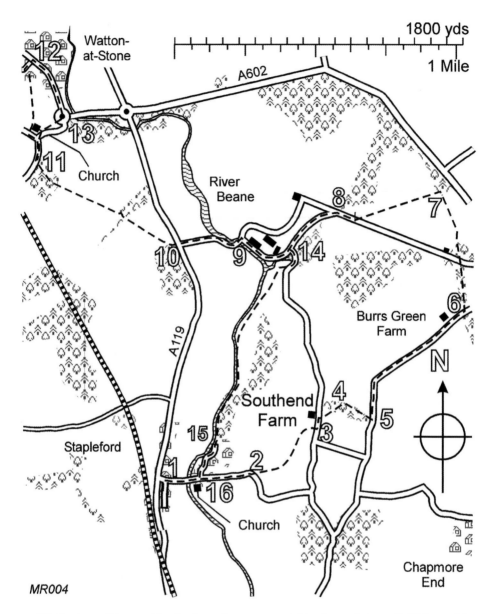

Watton-at-Stone

A602

River Beane

Church

A119

Burrs Green Farm

Southend Farm

Stapleford

N

Church

Chapmore End

MR004

Walk along this road for half a mile.

6. Go 100 yd beyond Burrs Green Farm and turn left down a narrow footpath through woodland to the driveway of an estate.
Cross the driveway near lodge gates and follow the footpath outside the estate wall. This wall is reputed to have been constructed by prisoners during the Napoleonic Wars.
Continue for a quarter mile, past metal steps attached to the wall, to a high wooden step-stile.

7. Climb the stile over the wall to enter Woodhall Park.
Follow a well-defined path straight out from the stile across open parkland until it joins the driveway after a quarter mile. Then turn right to follow the drive for 150 yd to a curving track on the left.

8. For the shorter 3.5 mile walk turn left to walk around the curve for 300 yd to a track on the left almost opposite the first farm buildings, and then continue from Point 14. For the complete walk, go right around the curve, then curve left with the River Beane on the left and farm building on the right.

9. At the junction beside the bridge over the river, turn left to follow the drive towards a gate and lodge on the A119.

10. Cross the road, enter the track opposite and after a few yards turn right along a footpath leading diagonally uphill across a field. Continue on a curving path through woods to emerge in another field with a plantation on the further side. Head straight across this field towards a gate that can be seen just left of some farm buildings. Carry on left of the buildings to reach Perrywood Lane.

11. Turn right and follow the lane down to Watton-at-Stone church and turn left at the junction by the church. Just beyond the churchyard, turn right on a narrow path between a fence and a hedge.

This path soon joins a tarmac path beside a gate into the churchyard. Turn left down this path between hedges and go past allotments and a playing field to emerge in a narrow lane.
Turn right along the lane, then right again into Watton-at-Stone High Street, with shops and public houses.

12. Turn right to go south along the High Street until the church can be seen up on the right.

13. Turn right up the footpath which leads to the churchyard and emerge on the lane with the church on the right.
Walk back up Perrywood Lane to rejoin your outward route and return past Points 11, 10 and 9 to reach Point 14.

14. Enter the track on the right that curves up to the left and near the end of the curve turn right on a footpath leading down across grass to a high step-stile.
Climb over this stile and follow a well-defined path running beside the River Beane.
Continue along this path for three-quarters of a mile until it reaches the end of a road called Clusterbolts.

15. Follow this road for a short distance until it reaches Church Lane opposite Stapleford church.

16. Turn right and follow the lane back to the start point.

5: Stapleford II – South to Hertford

This walk starts at Stapleford, a few miles north of Hertford on the A119, and climbs eastwards to Chapmore End on its way to Hertford. It returns along the River Beane footpath, part of the Hertfordshire Way.

OS Explorer 194, Land Ranger 166,
Distance: 7.5 miles (12 km),
Time: 4 hours,
A 4.5 mile (7.2 km) version is also shown.
Park: In service road beside A119 a quarter mile north of the railway bridge at Stapleford – SG14 3NW,

GR TL309169
Route: Footpaths, bridleways, quiet lanes and town pavements, paths may be muddy after rain, no climb-over stiles,
Access: Hertford Loop trains at Hertford North, and Buses Nos. 311, 372, 388, 390, Bus No. 390 at Stapleford, Refreshments: Public houses in Stapleford, Chapmore End and Hertford.

The St. Michael's Ramblers first walked this route, mostly in heavy rain, on May 29, 2010.

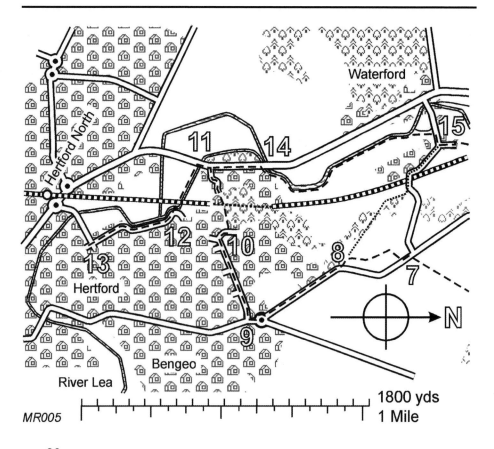

1. From the start point turn right into Church Lane to walk eastwards along a part of the Hertfordshire Way. Cross a narrow stream, then after 200 yd, cross the principal stream of the River Beane. Go past the church and primary school to climb following the lane and go round two sharp turns.
2. At the third sharp turn, to the right, walk straight on along a footpath crossing a field. Emerge in a lane at Stoneyhills and continue along the lane opposite.
3. After 250 yd, go through a gap in the hedge on the right, marked by a footpath sign, and follow a path with a hedge on the left.

Where this hedge almost meets a bluebell wood, turn left to stay on the path, still with a hedge on its left. Carry straight on for a third of a mile until the path emerges on the road at Chapmore End.
4. Turn right to follow the road and where the road turns sharp left, continue straight on along a wide track.
Then where this track starts to bear right, keep straight on past a path to the right followed soon after by another to the left. The track almost immediately disappears in a wide open area.
5. Turn left to follow a footpath along the left side of the area and carry on for more than a quarter mile. Cross a concrete drive and pass the site of old gravel machinery, then cross another concrete road and go down some steps into a wood.
6. At the foot of the steps, turn right to walk a twisting path that follows the edge of the wood, climbing away from the machinery site. Continue beyond the wood, along a narrow avenue of tall trees. After almost a third of a mile, the path passes beside houses to reach the Sacombe Road.
7. **Note: considerable traffic uses this road.**

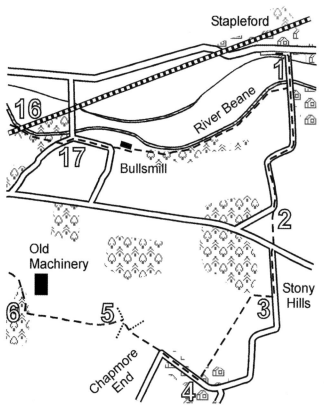

Stapleford

River Beane

16

17

Bullsmill

Old Machinery

6

5

Chapmore End

4

Stony Hills

2

3

Turn left for a few yards, then right through an N-shaped pinch stile into a nature park. Beyond the stile, go down a steep footpath with steps that finish on a cross path. Turn left to follow this path, curving along the bottom of the slope past a pond, and then eventually climbing to an exit from the park.

8. For the shorter 4.5 mile walk, turn back to the right and follow the path down to another exit on a lane beside a railway bridge. Turn left over this bridge and follow the lane for 800 yd to Barley Croft, then continue from Point 15.

   For the complete walk, leave the park to rejoin the Sacombe Road. Turn right, with a pavement after 100 yd, and go on to a roundabout on the Wadesmill Road.

9. Turn right, then right again into The Avenue to go past a school, and a small row of shops, then turn right into Cowpers Crescent.

10. After about eight houses opposite, turn left into a signed footpath between houses. Continue on this path that grows to a track, then a road winding downhill past houses to the A119 main road.

11. Turn left along the pavement, cross a small stream, then immediately turn left into a track beside the stream.

    Go under a high railway arch, past buildings on the right to emerge on Molewood Road.

12. Turn right along the road to enter Hertford at Port Vale. Refreshment may be obtained in Port Vale, or opposite Hertford North Station 300 yd to the right.

13. Return along Molewood Road and the track to the A119.

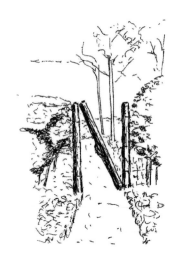

Turn right along the pavement, cross the first bridge and continue 400 yd to a second bridge over the River Beane.

14. Just before this bridge, turn right and follow a path past a weir to the open space of Waterford Marsh. Follow the riverside path for three-quarters of a mile until it bears away from the river to emerge on a lane opposite houses.

15. Turn right up the lane, then left into Barley Croft. At the far end, go through two gates and start along a footpath across a field to the river.

16. Follow this path under a railway arch through a wooded area to emerge on a lane and turn left along it.

17. After some yards, turn right up the lane towards Bulls Mill and continue straight on where the lane turns right. Beyond a large building on the left, turn left through a sign-posted gap to continue along the riverside path. Follow this path for a further half mile to emerge on Church Lane beside Stapleford church. Turn left and follow the lane back to the start point.

6: Archers Green to Hertingfordbury

This walk starts near Archers Green, north-east of Welwyn Garden City, and uses parts of the Hertfordshire Way. It crosses the River Mimram to climb the northern side of the valley, then descends into Hertingfordbury just west of Hertford and returns along the south side of the valley.

OS Explorer 182, Land Ranger 166,
Distance: 6.5 miles (10.4 km),
Time: 3¾ hours,
No shorter version is available,
Park: In lay-by beside B1000 a hundred yards east of Archers Green

Lane – SG14 2NQ, GR TL274134
Route: Footpaths, farm tracks, sections of grass verge and pavements beside lightly trafficked roads, paths may be muddy after rain, there are several climb-over stiles, the first stile does not have a dog gate,
Access: Bus 388 along B1000, and 380 to Hertingfordbury,
Refreshments: Public houses in Hertingfordbury.

The St. Michael's Ramblers first walked this route on August 8, 2011.

1. **Take care as the B1000 carries fast-moving traffic**. Cross the road, turn left and walk 100 yd along the grass verge. Turn right into Archers Green Lane and after a further 100 yd, climb over a stile on the right to follow a clearly defined path between the River Mimram and the road for 400 yd to a stone bridge.
2. Go over the bridge and follow the track to a gate stile. Continue straight up across a field and through another gate to follow a wide grassy track climbing between hedges. Go past several large houses on the left and an equestrian training area on the right to reach a lane.
3. Cross the lane and follow the path opposite with a wood on the right until a path leading right is reached just before a gate stile in the hedge ahead.
4. Turn right and follow the path between fences as it skirts Bacons Farm on the left to join the farm's tarmac drive.

5. Cross a lane and continue on a track that gradually narrows to a footpath. Follow the path for a mile across fields and through a wood until it reaches the B1000.
6. **Take care as this road carries fast traffic**. Turn left along the left-side grass verge of the road and continue for 250 yd to a footpath sign on the opposite side of the road.
7. Cross the road and follow a footpath diagonally to the left with a hedge on the right.

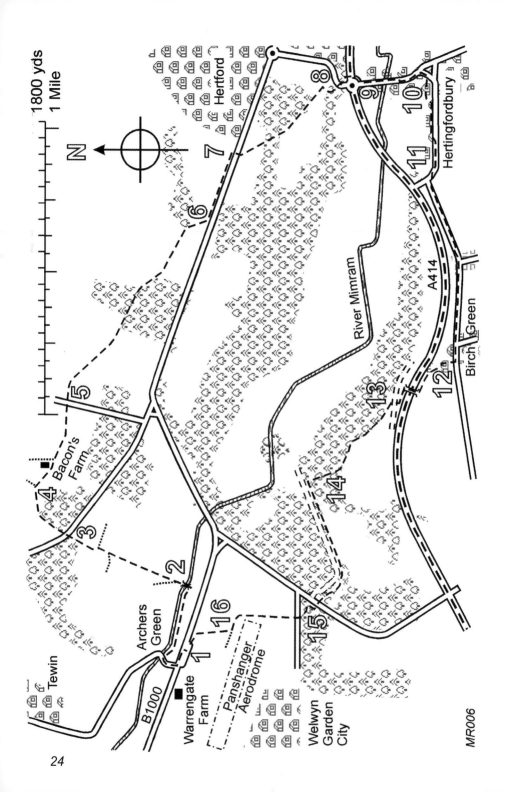

24

Continue past a plantation, through a wood and then with the wood on the left. Where the path divides, take the right branch which soon enters another wood. About 100 yd into the wood turn right down a steep slope to a car park. Bear left through the car park to emerge on a road (Thieves Lane).

8. **Take care as this road carries fast traffic**. Cross the road to walk down the pavement to a roundabout on the A414 dual carriageway road.

9. **Take care as the A414 road carries heavy traffic**. Follow the pavement to the left and cross both carriageways at the pedestrian crossing. Go right a few yards to enter Hertingfordbury Road and walk along the pavement, crossing a bridge over the River Mimram to pass a public house on the right.

10. At the second public house, turn right up a marked footpath beside it. This path runs behind the gardens of several houses and avoids a blind corner on the road, which now has no pavement. Where the path reaches a tarmac drive, turn left, then right immediately, to climb a path separated from the road by a hedge. Go past several houses to emerge beside the road. Continue on the pavement to the top of the hill.

11. Cross the road and enter the path opposite, with a hedge on the left and bushes on the right.
This path cuts off a corner to join the Old Coach Road and becomes a regular pavement. Where this ends, cross to the other side of the road and continue to the bus shelter at Birch Green.

12. At the bus shelter, turn right along a gravel drive marked by a footpath sign. After 50 yd, turn diagonally left to follow a path which goes through a fence and cuts across a private garden.
Where this path goes through a hedge, climb the stile and turn right beside the hedge. Then turn left beside a fence to cross a foot-bridge over the A414 and continue down the ramp to a substantial gravel track.

13. **Take care as this track carries heavy quarry machinery**. Cross the track and follow the path for half a mile with woods on the right. Keep right where the path divides and continue down a bracken-covered hill to a cross path identified as the Butterfield Path.

14. Turn left along this path and follow it beside a quarry track uphill for a little over half a mile. Continue beyond where the quarry track bears right for its separate exit and leave via a gate stile.

15. Cross Panshanger Road, go through the gate opposite and turn right, then left a few yards later beside another gate to enter a footpath to Panshanger Aerodrome.
Follow this path, across the aerodrome drive and continue with a hedge on the left past the end of the runway.

16. Continue round a bend to the left with trees on the left, until a clearly defined path starts downhill to the right. Go down this path and climb over a stile beside some trees. Continue down a smaller field, then enter more trees on the left and climb two final stiles to emerge beside the start point.

7:   High Cross to Cold Christmas – Return via Wadesmill

This walk starts at High Cross on Ermine Street north of Ware and crosses the A10 to visit Barwick Ford on the River Rib. It then follows the river path back via Cold Christmas to Wadesmill, from where it climbs again on its return to High Cross.

OS Explorer 194, Land Ranger 166,
Distance: 6 miles (9.7 km),
Time: 3¼ hours,
A 3.8 mile (6.1 km) version is also shown,
Park: On roads in High Cross –

SG11 1AN, GR TL363186,
Route: Farm and estate tracks, footpaths, quiet lanes and a short distance along pavements, paths may be muddy after rain, one climb-over stile and several notable hills,
Access: Buses No. 331 to High Cross,
Refreshments: Public houses in Wadesmill and High Cross.

The St. Michael's Ramblers first walked a version of this route on May 5, 2007.

1. Start from the junction between North Drive and the main north–south road through High Cross (Ermine Street). Walk along North Drive, past houses and over the bridge crossing the M10 dual carriageway road, then down a hill with fields to the left and woods on the right.
2. For the shorter walk, continue up the road which changes to a track, then bears right. Beyond the top of the hill, take the track angled left beside a wood (an arboretum), go straight downhill, cross a footbridge beside a ford, and turn right along the River Rib Path at Point 9.
   For the complete walk, go 100 yd beyond the ditch at the bottom of the hill, then turn left on a footpath across the field.
3. Turn right to follow the path uphill beside the field with woods on the left. Where the woods bear sharply away left, turn right along a gravel track beside a small airfield.
4. At the T-junction, turn left along the edge of a wood to follow the well-defined route of the Harcamlow Way for half a mile down to Great Barwick Manor. The Harcamlow Way is a long-distance footpath that follows a figure-eight route in Herts, Cambs and Essex.
5. Turn right at the manor and after a few yards join Gore Lane. Turn downhill and cross the footbridge beside a ford over the River Rib. Go beyond the furthest house on the right to a footpath leading into Sawtrees Wood on the right.
6. Enter the wood and continue along the path just inside the trees for a third of a mile. Then cross an open area before climbing up to join Cold Christmas Lane.
7. Turn right along the lane for a quarter of a mile, entering Cold Christmas to reach a track leading down to the right opposite a large house.
8. Go down this track between close hedges, ignoring another path to the left, and emerge in a field. Cross the field and turn left along the River Rib Path. Continue a quarter mile along this path and go past a footbridge and ford.

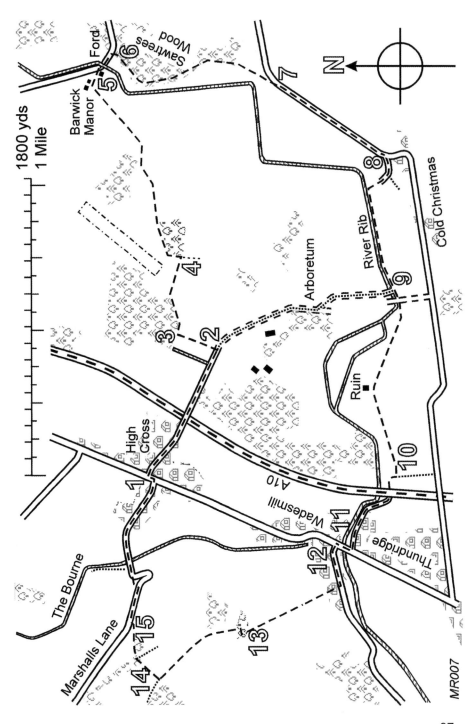

N

1800 yds
1 Mile

Ford

Sawtrees Wood

Barwick Manor

High Cross

Arboretum

River Rib

Cold Christmas

Ruin

A10

Wadesmill

Thundridge

The Bourne

Marshalls Lane

1
2
3
4
5
6
7
8
9
10
11
12
13
14
15

MR007

9. Beyond the ford the path winds past the entrance to a large house then enters a fenced gravel path (Church Lane). Continue along this path for three-quarters of a mile past a ruined church tower to reach a T-junction beside the A10 embankment.

10. Turn right and follow the path under the A10. Then bear right along a metalled lane into the lower end of Thundridge village beside Wadesmill.

11. Continue to the main road and turn right to cross the bridge over the river and enter Wadesmill village. Cross the main road into B158 Anchor Lane.

12. Walk along the pavement of Anchor Lane with houses on the right, and then turn right through a gap between houses on a footpath signed Sacombe 2.
Follow the path up between gardens and emerge in open fields. After some way, the path narrows and levels off; go straight on.

13. Pass through a small wood, hardly more than a thick hedge. Continue across an open field, then through a gap in a hedge to walk with a hedge on the right.
Follow the path through another gap in the hedge at the corner of the field to reach a footpath marker post at the corner of a wood on the left.

14. Turn right along a straight path and keep on for 250 yd to a junction of paths between the corners of two woods.
Turn half right and take the path that curves right with a wood on the right to reach Marshalls Lane.

15. Turn right, down the lane, taking the bridleway shortcut down to the left across the right loop of the lane, continuing for half a mile across a bridge over the Bourne and up a steep hill to return to the start point at High Cross.

8: Wadesmill – A Circular Walk North of the River Rib

This walk starts at Wadesmill north of Ware, climbing beside the surprisingly deep ravine of the Bourne while making a circuit on high land to the north visiting Sacombe church. The route was intended as a short winter walk to be completed without a break.

OS Explorer 194, Land Ranger 166,
Distance: 5 miles (8.0 km),
Time: 2¾ hours,
A 3.0 mile (4.8 km) version is also shown,
Park: On roads in Wadesmill – SG12 0TD, GR TL359175, **or with permission,** use the car park at either

public house.
Route: Farm or estate tracks and footpaths, there are several notable hills, no stiles; paths may be muddy after rain,
Beware: In places, the path beside the Bourne can have a drop of 60 ft down to the stream,
Access: Bus No. 331 to Wadesmill,
Refreshments: Public houses in Wadesmill.

The St. Michael's Ramblers first walked a version of this route on January 3, 2009.

1. Start from the junction between the B158 Anchor Lane and the main north–south road through Wadesmill, (Ermine Street). Walk northwards on the left-hand pavement beside Ermine Street for 150 yd to a private driveway with a footpath sign.
2. Turn left into the drive and follow a path towards a gate to the right of a garage.
   Go through the gate to a path with a deep, usually empty, water channel to the left (the Bourne). Soon afterwards cross a footbridge over to the left bank and carry on uphill.
3. Follow the path along a wooden terrace, then continue for more than half a mile to Marshalls Lane.
4. Turn left up the lane and then after 50 yd take the steep bridleway on the right crossing a left loop in the lane. Continue for 400 yd until the lane curves right. Take the footpath on the left and follow as it bears right beside trees.

5. At a junction of paths by marker posts where hedges meet, bear right from the centre post to a second post, then left on a straight path beside a double hedge on the left. After 250 yd, meet a cross path at the corner of a wood.
6. For the shorter walk, turn left to follow the path downhill for two-thirds of a mile and rejoin the route at Point 18.
   For the complete walk, turn right to walk with the wood on the left.
7. At the end of the wood, the path bears right becoming a gravel track. Follow this track through a small wood and past a house with an extensive walled garden.
8. Keep along the track as it makes lazy curves through another wood, emerging to become a tarmac road. Pass several houses on the left and a group of four oak trees on the right.
9. Just beyond the oaks, opposite a footpath marker post, turn right to follow a footpath straight across a

field towards the beautifully kept St. Catherine's Church, Sacombe.

10. From the church, turn left (south) to follow a gravel track uphill towards Sacombe Farm, where it becomes a tarmac road.

11. Continue along this road past other houses, crossing a cattle grid with a pedestrian gate beside it to go on past the "Way Out" sign for nearly half a mile.

12. Turn left on a concrete track by a marker post and a metal cabinet close to the hedge. Go through the gate stile to the right of the entrance to a covered reservoir and walk along part of the Hertfordshire Way on a wide grassy path to reach Bengeo Temple Farm.

13. At the nearest corner of the farm buildings, turn left through a gate stile and then immediately right along a path behind the buildings. Go over a small bridge to a gate stile by a larger footbridge and emerge on a farm track.

14. Turn left to follow it downhill into a small wood.

15. At the bottom of the hill, the track turns sharp left where another track joins from the right. Turn right for a few paces to a marker post, then go to the left up a steep path that becomes steps climbing out of the gully into a field.
Walk along the path with a hedge on the left and electric cables overhead. The path bears left still following the hedge which now has a wood behind it.

16. At the end of the field, the path turns right for a few paces before turning left through a gap beside the edge of the wood. Follow the path diagonally right across a field

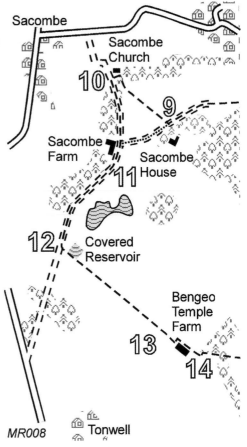

to cross a farm track and pass just right of Chelsing Farm. Continue straight on and soon there is a hedge to the left of the path.

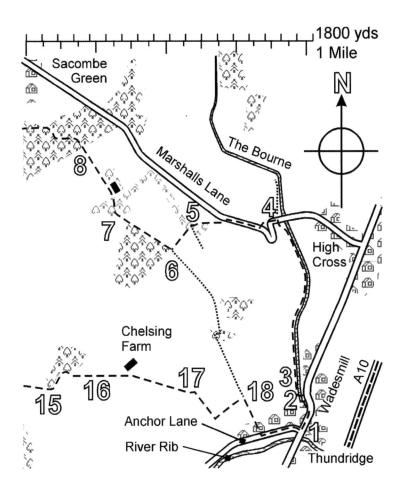

17. After a short climb, the path passes through a gap in a hedge and joins a path crossing it beside a solitary tree. Turn right to follow the power cables downhill, with the tower of Thunderidge church directly ahead. Soon after the cables bear away to the left, turn sharp left and walk along the old headland between fields.

18. Where this path ends at a T-junction by a "Puckish" group of trees (oak, ash and thorn) turn right downhill to Anchor Lane, then left to return to the start point.

9:   Wareside – A Circular Walk North to Cold Christmas

This short walk starts from Wareside, east of Ware, and visits Cold Christmas. It was intended as a winter walk that could be completed without a break.

OS Explorer 194, Land Ranger 166,
Distance: 4 miles (6.4 km),
Time: 2¼ hours,
No shorter version is shown,
Park: By the community hall in Wareside SG12 7QY, GR TL396156, **or with permission** use the car park at one of the public houses,
Route: Farm tracks and footpaths, paths may be muddy after rain, several hills and climb-over stiles,
Access: Buses No. M3 and M4 to Wareside,
Refreshments: Public houses in Wareside.

The St. Michael's Ramblers first walked this route on December 2, 2006.

1. Start from the junction between B1004 and the lane up to Bakers End. Walk up the signposted narrow footpath to the right of the house at the bottom left corner of the lane.
   Beyond the house, the path continues up a narrow gully along the course of a small stream. Where the path emerges on a lane, turn left for 50 yd until another lane joins from the right beside a school.
2. Turn right into the lane, and go through a gate stile immediately on the right and walk along a path signed for Newhall Green*.
   Carry straight on, through two more gates and a gap in a hedge. Continue on along the original line, towards a hedge corner on the opposite side of the field. Follow the path along the right of this hedge, then between hedges. Jink right through a gate and continue with a hedge on the left through a further gate.

This path may have been diverted via Babb's Green along a route similar to that shown dotted.

Pass to the right of converted farm buildings at New Hall Farm and emerge through yet another gate on to a lane.

3. Cross the lane and start along the wide track opposite that bends back to the left, ignoring the footpath leaving on the right. Continue along the track and pass two cottages on the left. Just beyond Legges Cottage, where the track makes a sharp left turn, turn right along a track between close hedges that leads towards a wood.
4. Keep straight on into the wood, continuing until the main track turns

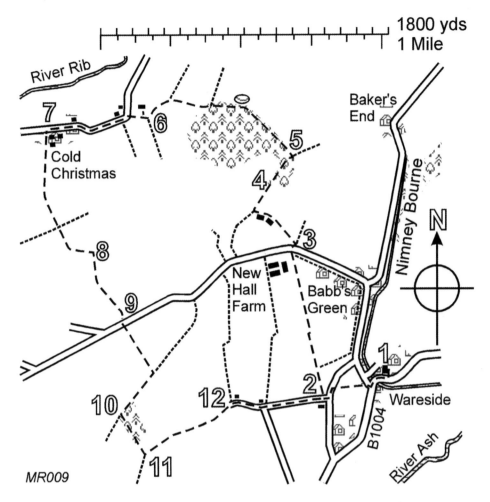

left where a lesser path leaves the far edge of the wood.

5. Follow the main track left as it runs just inside the wood, bearing left past a reservoir. Keep straight on where it emerges from the wood and follow the track as it winds along with a hedge on the right. Ignore a minor track to the right and continue to where three gravel tracks meet.

6. Take the right-hand track, ignoring another track on the right leading to the farm. Keep on as the route curves downhill through a gate in the hedge to emerge on the farm drive. Turn left along the drive for a few yards and left again into a lane. Continue along the lane past some houses on the right.

After 300 yd, reach the hamlet of Cold Christmas where there is a Meridian Line marker post on the left beside the road. Go on past larger houses on the left and beyond a Road Narrows sign.

33

7. Turn left up a steep concrete track marked "Swangles", continuing where it becomes a farm track along the edge of a field. As the slope levels out, follow the track left through a gap in the hedge. Soon afterwards, when there is good visibility, the towers of London City and Docklands can be seen away to the quarter right. Continue along the track, keeping straight on where a larger gravel track joins at a crossing.

8. Follow the track where it bears right by an oak tree at the start of a hedge, and continue on to reach a lane.

9. Cross the lane and start down a signed footpath opposite across a field. Go through a gap in the far hedge and on to a footpath running down the middle of the next field. Turn right to follow this path down through a hedge into the next field. Near the far end of this field, the path runs down along the right side of a small wood.

10. At the bottom of the wood, turn left along a path that runs just inside the trees.

11. After 300 yd, this path meets a cross path. Turn left up a "hollow way" between hedges. This way gains a tarmac surface after 400 yd and passes between several large houses to emerge on the tight bend of a lane.

12. Continue straight on along the lane until the school is reached at a T-junction (Point 2). Turn left, then after 50 yd turn right and return down the narrow gully to the start point at Wareside.

10: Stanstead Abbots – North Over the Hill to Wareside

This walk climbs over high ground north of the River Lea using part of the Hertfordshire Way. It starts from Stanstead Abbots, across the river from St. Margarets south of Ware, and visits Wareside.

OS Explorer 194, Land Ranger 166,
Distance: 6 miles (9.7 km),
Time: 3¼ hours,
A 4 mile (6.4 km) version is also shown,
Park: Public car park off the High Street at Stanstead Abbots – SG12 8AS GR TL384119,

Route: Pavements, estate and farm tracks, short sections on country lanes, several strenuous hills, no climb-over stiles, paths may be muddy after rain,
Access: Buses No. 311, 351, 524, C3 and East Hertford Line trains, to St. Margarets,
Refreshments: Public houses, restaurants and cafes in Stanstead Abbots and St. Margarets, two public houses at Wareside.

The St. Michael's Ramblers first walked this route on October 3, 2009.

1. Turn left out of the car park and walk eastwards along the High Street.
2. At the roundabout, turn left and follow the road towards Ware. Cross this road to walk along the continuous pavement on the far side.
   Follow the road past a large church and several marked footpaths to reach the final houses in the town beside a brick-enclosed pillarbox.
3. Turn up the narrow path on the right just before a tarmac drive enters the grounds of Easneye College. Follow this path as it climbs between hedges, then widens into a track and the right-hand hedge gives way to open fields.
4. After half a mile, go through a gate across the track, and carry straight on past houses and outside dog pens. Follow the track as it curves down through woodland to emerge between open fields approaching Hall Ford.
5. Cross the footbridge over the River Ash beside the ford.
   For the shorter walk, turn right on the path along an old railway track. Keep on for 250 yd to reach a house on the right-hand side. Turn right up a steep track just before the house for 300 yd until another path comes from the left. This is the path noted in Point 14. Continue **straight on**, less steeply, to woods and fields that are described from Point 15 onwards.

For the complete walk, cross the former railway track and walk up a tarmac road between farm buildings to reach the B1004 road between Ware and Bishop's Stortford.

6. Cross the B1004 to continue along a farm track almost opposite leading to Newhole and Swades Farms.

7. Just before the track enters the garden of a house, turn right and follow a narrow hedged track between gardens.
   After a short distance cross a small stream that is often dry, then climb up through a small patch of woodland. Ignore other paths which diverge from the track and continue along a "hollow way" between hedges.

8. After a quarter mile, the track gains a tarmac surface and passes between several large houses to emerge on the tight bend of a lane. Continue straight on along the lane until a school is reached at a T-junction.

9. Turn left and then after 50 yd, turn right to descend a path down a narrow gully following the course of

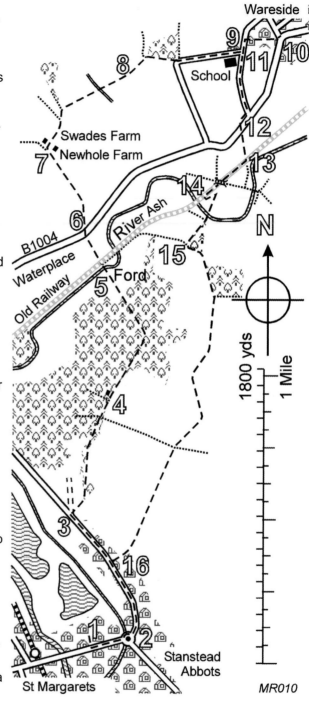

a small stream. The path emerges beside a house at Wareside.

10. Turn right to reach the main through road (B1004). There are public houses on either side of the road here. After three miles of walking, either could be a good place to break for refreshment. Return to the path beside the house, and climb back up the gully to the lane.

11. **Be aware that traffic uses this lane.** Turn left to follow the lane for a quarter mile until it reaches the B1004.

12. Stay on the nearer side of the road for better traffic visibility. Turn right to walk along it for 50 yd, then cross over to enter a concrete track that runs downhill.

13. At the bottom, beside a handsome brick house, turn right on a wide path that follows an old railway track. After a 100 yd this path passes under a bridge. Then after a further 70 yd, another path runs obliquely back on the left.

14. Turn left and walk back along this path for 20 yd until a marker post is seen on the left opposite a path that leaves to the right. Turn right to follow this path across the field towards a footbridge over the river. This is part of the Hertfordshire Way.

Cross the bridge, pass between bushes and then to the right of a cottage. Continue up along a wider track past woods on the left and a broad gully nearby among the trees. After 200 yd, the path ends at a cross track.

15. Turn left to follow the track which continues less steeply uphill, still with woods on the left. The way soon levels off between fields with fine views to the south and west. Ignore all other paths to follow the track for a mile and descend between houses to emerge on the road from Stanstead Abbots described in Point 2.

16. Turn left and follow the pavement back into the town. Again cross the road by the roundabout and walk back along the High Street to the start point at the car park.

11: Stanstead Abbots II – Two Rivers to Hoddesdon

This walk in the Lea Valley follows parts of the River Stort and River Lea tow paths. Starting from Stanstead Abbots, just across the River Lea from St. Margarets, south of Ware, it touches Roydon and visits Dobb's Weir and Rye House.

OS Explorer 174/194, Land Ranger 166/167,
Distance: 7 miles (11.2 km),
Time: 3¾ hours,
A 5.2 mile (8.3 km) version is also shown,
Park: Public car park off the High Street at Stanstead Abbots – SG12 8AS GR TL384119
Route: Level town pavements, footpaths and river towpaths, paths may be muddy after rain or during high water levels, no climb-over stiles,
Access: Buses No. 311, 351, 524, C3 and East Hertford Line trains, to St. Margarets,
Refreshments: Public houses, restaurants and cafes in Stanstead Abbots, St. Margarets, Dobb's Weir and Rye House.

The St. Michael's Ramblers first walked this route on May 2, 2009.

---

1. Turn left out of the car park, to walk eastwards along the High Street. At the roundabout, turn right and follow the road towards Roydon.
2. Where this bears left up a hill, keep right along Netherfield Lane. Go on past where the tarmac changes to gravel and then on to a tunnel beneath the A414 Hertford to Harlow main road.

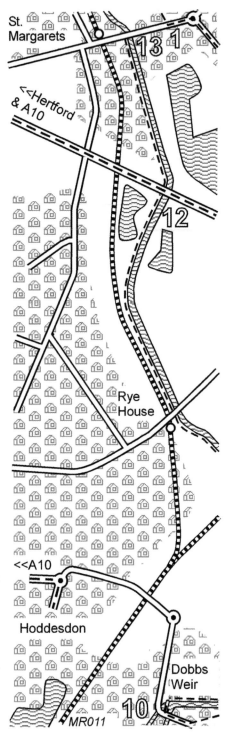

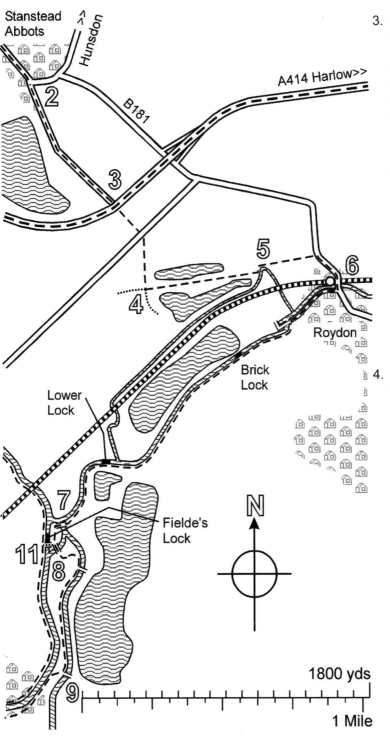

Stanstead Abbots

Hunsdon

2

3

B181

A414 Harlow>>

5

6

4

Roydon

Brick Lock

Lower Lock

7

Fielde's Lock

11

8

9

N

1800 yds

1 Mile

3. Go through the tunnel, ignore a sign to the right and go straight on along a path by a hedge to a minor road. Cross this road and follow a path going diagonally right (due south). Continue 300 yd to an area where several grassy paths converge.

4. At the single wooden power pole, turn left (east) along a wide grassy way, following power cables. Where the track bears right, go straight on following the cables towards a gate. There are actually three gates, so take the centre metal

one and go straight on along a narrow path to a bend in a small river – the original course of the River Stort.

5. Turn left to follow the river bank round, and then continue eastwards along the path straight across open fields, with Stanstead Bury church visible in trees to the left. At the Roydon Road turn right and then cross the Stanstead Airport and Harlow railway line on a level crossing beside Roydon station.

6. Cross the River Stort navigation by a bridge to enter Essex and turn right along the road beside the "navigation".

   Just before Roydon Mill, where the road rises for a bridge, turn left along the towpath. After a third of a mile pass Brick Lock, go another half mile to Lower Lock and then a final third of a mile to Fielde's Weir and Lock at the confluence of the Rivers Stort and Lea.

7. At the weir, go left and immediately right to cross the long bridge over the weir itself. Follow the wide track to the left and after a short distance see a track to the right leading to a bridge over the River Lea, with three stacks of a small power station beyond it.

8. For the shorter walk, cross this bridge, turn right and go north along the River Lea towpath back to St. Margarets as described from Point 11.

   For the complete walk, continue along the wide track, over another bridge and round to the left where it stays wide enough for motor traffic. The track turns sharp right to run along the west side of a broad channel. Despite this being "a traffic-free cycle route", cycles are unlikely to be seen here. Follow this track, passing a wide bridge on the left, then after a further third of a mile reach a footbridge on the left.

9. Just past the bridge by a large power pylon on the right, turn beyond the pylon to follow a narrow path heading diagonally towards the River Lea. Go along the path which leads into a public garden. Leave the garden by a gate on to the Dobb's Weir Road. Turn right and after a few yards pass a public house on the right, with a cafe opposite.   After 4 miles of walking, this could be a good time to break for refreshment.

10. Follow the road across a bridge over the navigation, immediately turning right to walk down and across a footbridge just above Dobb's Weir. Turn right along the River Lea towpath to walk north one mile to Fielde's Lock.

11. Continue 300 yd beyond the lock and go under a railway bridge. On the far side of the river, at Rye House, are a go-kart track, a public house and the remains of Rye House gateway. Follow the tow-path northwards for three-quarters of a mile.

12. Go under the bridge carrying the A414 between Hertford and Harlow. Continue a further half mile, past riverside houses, to the bridge at St. Margarets.

13. At the bridge, follow the path up from the towpath and turn right along the High Street to return to the start point in the car park.

12: A Short Walk from Essendon on the Lea Valley Path

This very short walk from Essendon, east of Hatfield, follows part of the Lea Valley Walk. It was an early group ramble intended to encourage non-walkers to take part, being short enough to complete without a break.

OS Explorer 182, Land Ranger 166,
Distance: 3.5 miles (5.6 km),
Time: 2 hours,
Park: Beside the sports field on Essendon High road or in School Lane

opposite – AL9 6HD, GR TL275086,
Route: Pavements, estate tracks, footpaths, no climb-over stiles, two notable hills, paths may be muddy after rain,
Access: Buses No. 200, 201 and 341,
Refreshments: Public houses in Essendon and at Essendon West End.

The St. Michael's Ramblers first walked this route on May 15, 2004.

1. From the sports field, go north, bearing left to pass to the right of the church.
2. At the T-junction, turn left, then just beyond the last house on the right, turn right through a gate stile. Follow the footpath sign diagonally right across the field, down towards a power pole near the far corner.
3. Emerge on Essendon High Street and cross to the pavement on the far side. Turn left and walk downhill.

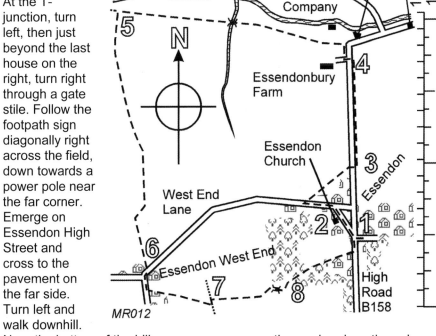

4. Near the bottom of the hill, opposite the entrance to Essendonbury Farm (which a safe Distance from the sharp corner)

cross the road and continue down along the grass verge.
Enter the signed bridleway right on the apex of the bend. This is part of

the Lea Valley Walk. Follow the bridleway for just over three-quarters of a mile to a wide track leading uphill to the left, Cross a bridge over a small stream about halfway along.

5. Turn left uphill. This track climbs about 130 ft in the first three-quarters of a mile, then after almost another quarter of a mile emerges on a corner of West End Lane with a public house almost opposite.

6. Cross to the public house and go down the left side on a path leading downhill with a hedge on the left. Continue down the edges of two fields and through a hedge to emerge on a cross path.

7. Turn left then immediately right to continue across another field beside a hedge on the left.

8. Cross a footbridge, then follow a winding path, taking a right turn uphill to tunnel into woodland. Climb steeply through woods, then beside a paddock to a gate at the corner of a sports field.
Go through the gate, keep along the edge of the field and then through another gate back to Essendon High Road close to the start point.

13: Broxbourne to Rye House and Dobb's Weir

Starting from Broxbourne Mill on the River Lea south of Ware, this walk visits Rye House, returning via Dobb's Weir. It was intended as an easy winter walk in other seasons the shorter route is a good family walk as there is usually some river activity.

OS Explorer 194, Land Ranger 166,
Distance: 5 miles (8 km),
Time: 2¾ hours,
A 3.5 mile (5.4 km) version is also shown,
Park: Broxbourne Mill or picnic site car parks, on Church Lane, beside St. Augustine's Church in Broxbourne –

EN10 7JX, GR TL372069
Route: Pavements, towpaths and footpaths, paths may be muddy after rain or during high water levels, no climb-over stiles,
Access: East Hertford line trains to Broxbourne and Rye House, Buses No. 310, 311, 323, 324, and C3,
Refreshments: Public houses and cafes at Broxbourne Mill, Rye House and Dobb's Weir.

The St. Michael's Ramblers first walked the shorter version of this route on December 5, 2005 and the longer version on November 6, 2010.

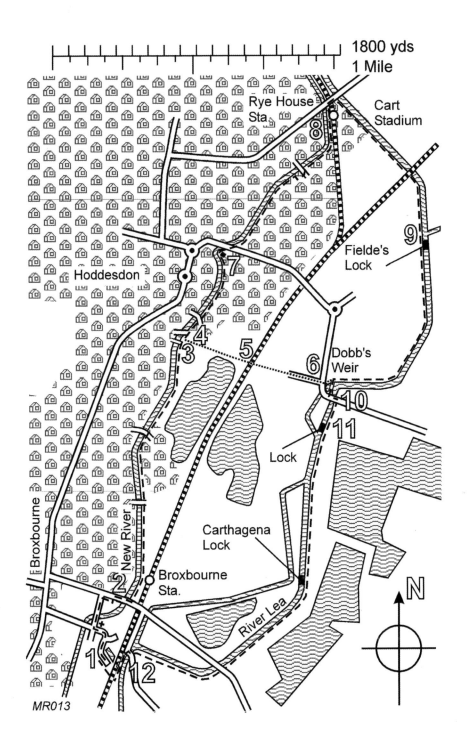

1800 yds
1 Mile

Rye House Sta.

Cart Stadium

8

Fielde's Lock

9

Hoddesdon

7

4

3

5

6

Dobb's Weir

10

11

Lock

Carthagena Lock

Broxbourne

New River

Broxbourne Sta.

2

River Lea

1

12

N

MR013

43

1. Walk up Church Lane and turn right beyond the church into Churchfields. Continue past the churchyard and cross a bridge over the "New River".
   This fast-flowing stream is neither new nor a river, but is actually an artificial channel opened in 1613 to supply fresh water to a growing London.
   Continue beyond the bridge, then turn right beside the main road. **Take care: this road carries heavy traffic**. Cross the road at the light-controlled crossing and turn right on the pavement to go back over the New River.

2. At the far side of the bridge, turn left on to the grassy New River Path, with water on the left and house gardens beyond. Go past Broxbourne station where the path gains a gravel surface and walk on with larger houses on the far side. Continue through several sets of gate stiles past more bridges for three-quarters of a mile to a grassy area with a lake beyond on the right, a narrow footbridge on the left and a road bridge close ahead.

3. For the shorter walk, go to Point 4. For the complete walk, go on past several bridges to a main road just beyond a sharp bend where the path squeezes between the "river" and an old pump house, then continue from Point 7.

4. Turn right beyond the narrow bridge and go through a gate stile with a sign for Dobb's Weir. Walk down a path with gardens on the left and continue through another gate stile into a nature area to reach a railway crossing.

5. **TAKE GREAT CARE to observe all instructions as this line**

carries **FREQUENT STANSTED EXPRESS TRAINS.** Cross the railway line and follow the path starting with stepping stones, progressing to a wide concrete road with industrial units to the left and ending at a main road.

6. Cross the main road to the footpath opposite and go over a small concrete bridge. Turn left on a path with the River Lea on the right. Ignoring the first footbridge over Dobb's Weir itself, cross the grass past weir machinery to a second longer bridge upstream of the weir. Cross this bridge, with a public house over the river, go up to the road, and continue from Point 10.

7. At the main road beside the New River, **take care – this is Essex Road which carries heavy industrial traffic**.
   Cross the road and follow the river path outside the railings. Approach the next bridge well to the right of the railings to get to the gate stile, and then continue along the path.

8. When Rye House railway station is seen on the right, leave the path at the next bridge and turn right on a road with no pavement. Then on pavement, go over the railway and turn right into a residential area just before a third bridge goes over the River Lea.
   Cross the road and take a tarmac path down to the river. Turn right along the towpath and follow it for three-quarters of a mile, past a go-kart stadium on the far side, to the confluence with the River Stort at Fielde's Lock.

9. Continue along the River Lea for three-quarters of a mile to Dobb's Weir. Turn left over the footbridge just upstream of the weir, with a

public house opposite. Then climb up to the road.

10. Turn left and cross the "navigation" on the narrow pavement of an elevated road bridge. There is a cafe opposite the public house. Cross the road immediately beyond the bridge and walk down the path between "navigation" and car park to follow the towpath 250 yd to Dobb's Weir Lock.

11. Continue beside the river for half a mile past a large lake and track on the left, to Carthagena Lock. Carry on along the towpath for another half mile where the river bends right and goes under a road bridge.

Keep on past a swimming pool opposite to see boats moored on the far side on the approach to Broxbourne.

12. Go past a public house on the left and climb steps to a road. Turn right and recross the river on the even narrower pavement of another elevated road bridge. Beyond the bridge, cross the road and turn left down steps to continue along the towpath. Follow the towpath, over a footbridge and just after the bridge, turn right to go under the railway line and emerge at the bottom end of Mill Lane to return to the start point.

14: Little Berkhamsted to Essendon

This walk was originally conceived as a shady ramble for a hot summer's day. The route mostly uses tree-lined estate and farm tracks in the Little Berkhamsted area following parts of the Hertfordshire Way.

OS Explorer 194, Land Ranger 166,
Distance: 6.8 miles (10.9 km),
Time: 3¾ hours (more in hot weather),
No shorter version is available,
Park: Lay-by beside the cricket field on Church Road, Little Berkhamsted – SG13 8LY, GR TL292078,
Route: Farm tracks, footpaths, short sections on country lanes, several hills – one steep, paths may be muddy after rain, no climb-over stiles,
Access: Buses No. 308 and 380 to Little Berkhamsted, 200, 201 and 341 to Essendon,
Refreshments: public houses in Essendon, Little Berkhamsted and Essendon West End.

The St. Michael's Ramblers first walked a version of this ramble on July 6, 2006.

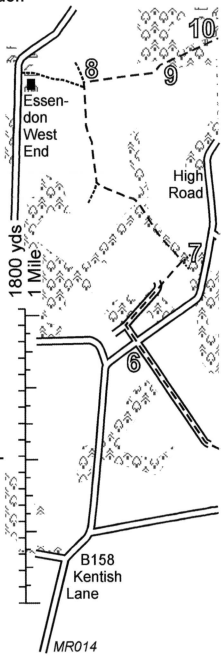

---

1. Turn left through a gate near the north end of the lay-by and start along the right side of the cricket field. Exit through another gate and turn left on a bridleway. After half a mile, kink right as a track comes from the left. The route becomes a tarmac lane with houses on either side. Go past a water tower and two high antennae.
2. Where the lane starts to bear left, turn right beside a brick wall opposite a footpath sign, and follow the gravel drive of a large house. Keep to the right of the house and

enter a narrow path that follows the same line. Carry on and after a

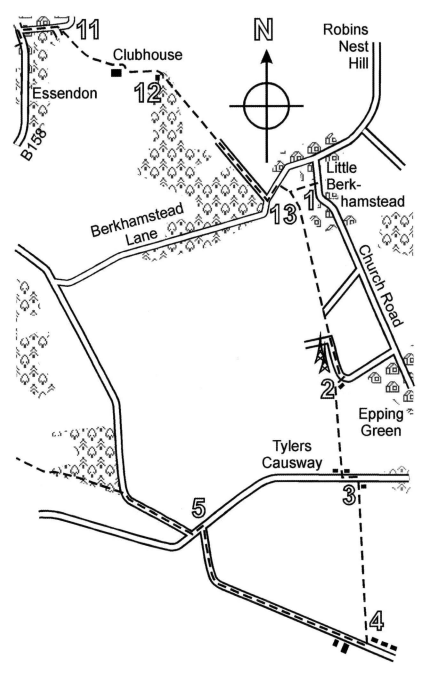

N

Robins
Nest
Hill

Clubhouse

Essendon

B158

11

12

Little
Berk-
hamstead

Berkhamstead
Lane

13

1

Church Road

2

Epping
Green

Tylers
Causway

5

3

4

short distance turn right through a
gate in a hedge. Turn left to follow

a fenced path. Continue for a
quarter mile through several more

47

gates to pass left of a garden wall and emerge in a road.

3. **Take care: this road carries fast-moving traffic**. Cross the road, turn left to go 100 yd to an opening on the right just before a house. Walk through the opening and take a path running along the edge of a field. Follow the path with a hedge to the left for half a mile until it enters a thicket. The path soon goes between two houses and comes out on a tarmac lane.

4. Turn right to follow this lane, past a large farm, where it becomes a track. Continue for three-quarters of a mile to a road.

5. **Take care: this road carries fast-moving traffic**. Cross the road, turn left to walk 100 yd and enter Cucumber Lane on the right. Follow the lane for a quarter mile until a marked path leads off to the left (Hornbeam Lane). Follow this three-quarters of a mile to a road.

6. Cross the road and enter a gated drive that ends at a cross track after 100 yd. Turn right and follow the track for more than a quarter of a mile. Keep straight on both where the major track turns left and where the lesser track also turns left and the route becomes a grassy footpath. Continue downhill between fields into woodland.

7. Turn left where the path reaches a cross path by a marker post, with a footbridge just beyond on the right. Follow this path through woods beside a stream for a third of a mile until it joins a track coming from the left. Turn right downhill along the new track.

8. After 300 yd, a path comes down from the left that may be followed for 300 yd to a public house at

Essendon West End. Otherwise continue a few yards further on the original path and then turn right into a field to go downhill with a hedge on the left.

9. Cross a footbridge and follow a winding path that turns uphill to tunnel among bushes. The path climbs steeply straight on through woods, then beside a paddock to a gate at the corner of a sports field. Keep along the edge of the field and go through another gate to Essendon High Road. There is a public house 100 yd in either direction. Either could be a good break for refreshment.

10. From the sports field, turn left for a few yards, then cross the road to enter School Lane. Go on for about 150 yd past a community hall, and then turn right by a driveway.

11. Start along the footpath just to the left of the gate post. After 150 yd, the path becomes a narrow road across a golf course. Follow the roadway past the clubhouse where it curves right then left downhill. Continue on to a white cottage to the right of the route where several tracks meet.

12. Take the track that goes left round the cottage and climbs to the right behind it. Continuing uphill, the gradient levels off between fields. Go past farm buildings, a small duck pond and a house to the lane just beyond.

13. Turn left up the lane for 100 yd and then right into a bridleway. After less than 200 yd, turn left into a cricket field. Keep to the left of the cricket field and exit through the further gate to return to the start point.

15: Holyfield to Waltham Abbey

This walk in the Lea Valley Regional Park starts from the Lea Valley Park Farms Visitor Centre at Holyfield south of Nazeing. The route passes lakes full of water birds beside the River Lea to visit Waltham Abbey, returning via a dragonfly sanctuary.

OS Explorer 194, Land Ranger 166
Distance: 6 miles (9.7 km),
Time: 3¼ hours,
Park: At the Visitor Centre off Holyfield Road (B194) south of Nazeing –
EN9 2EF, GR TL382034,
A 4.4 mile (7.0 km) route starts from Fishers Green – EN9 2EF, TL376029,

Route: Tarmac footpaths, field paths, a quarter mile of pavement, paths may be muddy after rain or during high water levels, gentle gradients up, one steeper hill down, no climb-over stiles,
Access: Trains to Waltham Cross, Buses No. 555 along Holyfield Rd, 211, 212, 213, 240, 250, 251 and 555 serve Waltham Abbey,
Refreshments: Tea room at the Visitor Centre, public houses and cafes at Waltham Abbey.

The St. Michael's Ramblers first walked this 100th ramble on May 5, 2012.

---

1. For the shorter 4.4 mile route, follow Points 3 to 14 from Fishers Green car park a quarter mile south of the Holyfield turning. For the complete walk, leave the Visitor Centre car park on a path at the opposite corner from the Centre. Soon turn left at a T-junction and follow the path as it passes a bird-feeding centre to emerge in a second car park. Go diagonally left through this car park
2. Enter a footpath beside a picnic area and keep on across one of the many streams of the River Lea to a viewing area overlooking Seventy Acres lake. Turn left to follow a path between the lake and the river in a semi-circle route, then sharp right to a third car park beside a bridge at Fishers Green.
3. Take the straight path to the right beside the lake and go a quarter of a mile to a path on the left.
4. Turn left along this twisty path between two lakes to a T-junction beyond them.

5. Turn right towards the "navigation" on its embankment. Just before the embankment, turn right over a foot-bridge across a ditch, climb up to Waltham Common lock and turn left over the footbridge by the lock.
6. If the towpath is uncrowded, turn left along it for three-quarters of a mile past Waltham Town lock and go under the main road. However, should the towpath be really crowded (perhaps with cyclists), take the quieter path diagonally left that goes past Bowyer's Water and rejoin the towpath further along, turning right to continue on to the lock then under the road bridge.
7. Beyond the bridge, climb back up to the main road and turn right along the pavement towards Waltham Abbey a quarter of a mile away. The town is well provided with public houses and cafes so is a suitable place for refreshment.
8. Turn left across the main entrance of the Abbey church to follow the

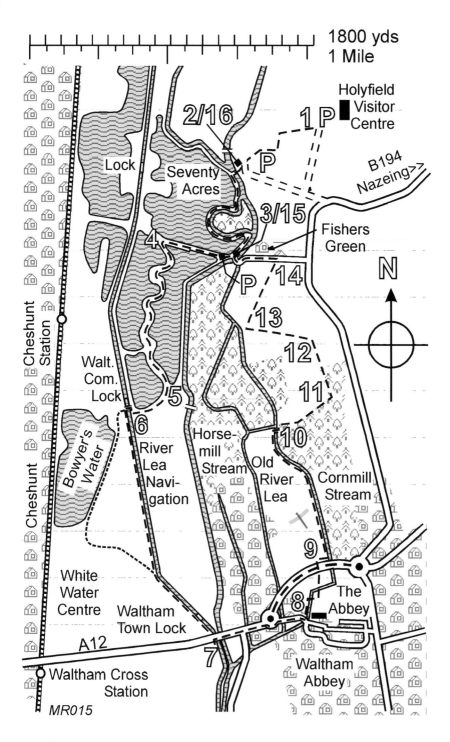

1800 yds
1 Mile

Holyfield
Visitor
Centre

2/16

1 P

P

B194
Nazeing>>

Lock

Seventy
Acres

3/15

Fishers
Green

N

4

P

14

13

12

11

Cheshunt Station

Walt.
Com.
Lock

5

Bowyer's Water

6

River
Lea
Navi-
gation

Horse-
mill
Stream

Old
River
Lea

Cornmill
Stream

10

Cheshunt

9

White
Water
Centre

Waltham
Town Lock

8

The
Abbey

A12

7

Waltham
Abbey

Waltham Cross
Station

path beside a stream north through the Abbey grounds. After 100 yd turn right under a ruined arch towards the Abbey Information Centre, then left to pass beside it.

Continue over a bridge, then under the ring road and straight on though a gate.

9. Turn right inside water meadows then left beside the Cornmill stream. Follow this stream for about half a mile to a bridge on the right.

10. Turn right over the bridge, left for a few yards, then right again to go 400 yd up a gently climbing path, with a high fence on the left and conifers on its right.

11. Continue beside the fence after it turns left for another 400 yd.

12. Where the fence turns left again, follow a path running diagonally left down across an open field.

13. Turn right and go along a path towards the nearer end of a hedge, then continue beside the hedge to emerge on a lane.

14. Turn left along the lane, over a metal bridge to the Fishers Green car park mentioned in Point 2.

Turn right to return along the path between lake and river, going back around the semi-circle to the viewing area. Turn right and return past the picnic site to the second car park.

15. Go straight on across this car park and return along the tarmac path back to first car park and the start point.

16: Brookmans Park to North Mymms

This walk explores partially isolated countryside near the A1(M) at Water End south of Hatfield that is usually missed by car travellers.

OS Explorer 194, Land Ranger 166,
Distance: 4.6 miles (7.4 km),
Time: 2¾ hours,
Park: On roads near Brookmans Park railway station –
AL9 7SS, GR TL241041,
A shorter 2.2 mile (3.5 km) route is also included starting from St. Mary's Church, North Mymms –
AL9 7TW, GR TL222045

Route: Estate and farm tracks, footpaths, short sections on country lanes, one large flight of steps (up and down), paths may be muddy after rain, no climb-over stiles,
Access: Buses No. 201, 202, 302, 610 to Brookmans Park, 200, 304, 312 to North Mymms, Trains to Brookmans Park,
Refreshments: public houses and cafes at Water End and Brookmans Park.

The St. Michael's Ramblers first walked this route on May 2, 2004.

---

1. For the short 4.4 mile route, start at St. Mary's Church and follow Points 9 to 12 and then 4 to 9. For the complete walk start from the railway bridge beside Brookmans Park Station. Walk down the paved path at the far side of the bridge from the shops towards the old booking office and the ticket machine. Carry on past these and the footbridge for the platforms to a footpath beside the railway line. Continue along this path with a fence on the left for a quarter mile to a long set of steps descending the embankment to the right.

2. Go down the steps and start along a path with a hedge on its right running almost straight out from the railway. Follow this path through a section with hedge on one side and fence on the other over fields for a quarter mile. Carry on beside a stream across more fields, past a single gate stile on the right, to several gate stiles together near the corner of a wood.

Turn right through the first stile, cross a bridge over the stream, leave via another stile and turn left to cross a track and go through a third stile into the wood.

3. Follow the path through the wood with the stream close by on the left. Motorway noise starts to become noticeable, unfortunately it may continue for the next half hour. Carry on 300 yd beyond the wood, eventually following a duckboard section that first crosses the stream, then the Mimmshall Brook, to reach Warrengate Road.

4. Turn left (south) along the road for more than a quarter mile, past a flood protection wall on the left and houses on the right to cross roads beside flood gates.

5. Turn right and walk up a narrow road to a major road (Swanland Road) running parallel with the A1(M) motorway.

6. **Take care: Swanland Road carries fast-moving traffic.** Cross the road to the path opposite and follow this round the approach to a

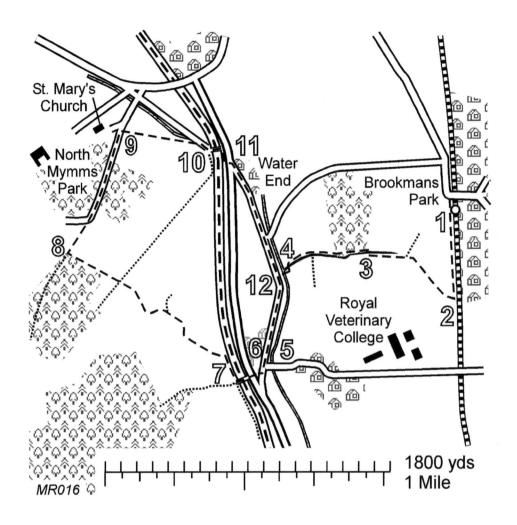

St. Mary's Church

North Mymms Park

Water End

Brookmans Park

Royal Veterinary College

8

9

10

11

12

4

3

2

1

6

5

7

1800 yds
1 Mile

MR016

footbridge and continue over the motorway. At the far side, walk a few yards through a pinch stile to a cross path.

7. Turn right and follow this winding path, leaving the motorway after a few yards to continue for three-quarters of a mile. Pass two un-surfaced tracks to the right, then woods, to a third track with a gravel surface.

8. Turn right and follow this track, to a gate on to the drive for North Mymms Park. Continue a third of a mile to a turning on the left leading to St. Mary's Church with a signed footpath and gate stile opposite.

9. Go through the gate stile and follow this path across fields to emerge by steps leading up the approach to a footbridge over the motorway.

10. Follow this path to the right to re-cross the motorway and go down a long path between tight hedges to emerge on Swanland Road again

at Water End by the junction with Warrengate Road. There is a cafe opposite, and a public house a few yards further along Warrengate Road, both opportunities for refreshment.

11. **Take care: Swanland Road carries fast-moving traffic**. Cross to Warrengate Road and turn right to follow it past houses.
Continue for a third of a mile to where the path from Brookmans Park emerges from over the river in Point 5.

12. Go back across the river and return along the footpath past Points 4, 3, 2 to 1 and the start point.

17: Salisbury Hall and River Colne

This walk, mostly on firm pathways south of London Colney, was conceived as a winter walk to be completed without a break. The route skirts Salisbury Hall and returns beside the River Colne.

OS Explorer 194, Land Ranger 166,
Distance: 4.1 miles (6.6 km),
Time: 2¼ hours,
No suitable shorter route is suggested,
Park: In the public car park on Riverside, east of High Street near the bridge over the River Colne – AL2 1QA, GR TL182037.

Route: Estate and farm tracks, field and riverside paths, plus short section on pavements, gentle slopes, 30 steps up, paths may be muddy after rain, one climb-over stile,
Access: Buses No. 84, 359, 602 and 632 to London Colney,
Refreshments: Restaurants and cafes at Colney Fields Retail Park, public houses and cafes in London Colney.

The St. Michael's Ramblers are scheduled to walk this route on February 8, 2014.

1. Leave the car park and at the end of Riverside, cross High Street and descend a few steps to Waterside. Follow the pavement on the left for 100 yd as it bears right between the river and a public house to a footpath with a sign for Bell Lane.
2. Turn left on this path, immediately crossing a footbridge over the river, followed shortly by a cross path. Continue straight on for 50 yd to a gate stile by a hedge. Go through the stile and carry on 200 yd and go past another cross path to some shallow steps.
3. Continue straight on up the steps and carry on 400 yd along a path behind a supermarket to the M25 motorway. Turn right and climb 30 steps to turn left on a path over a footbridge crossing the motorway and continue on to Bell Lane.
4. Cross Bell lane, ignoring the footpath sign opposite and go left along the pavement for 150 yd to the drive into Watford FC grounds. Turn into this drive (local Walk 25) and climb over the stile by the gate

keeper's kiosk to follow the drive for half a mile, past a roundabout and sports club to a cross track.
5. Turn right on this track for 20 yd, then left again to continue, parallel with the original line, along a grassy path for another 200 yd, then through a gap in a hedge to a wide concrete track.
6. Turn left along this track towards Salisbury Hall, which is where the prototype de Havilland Mosquito fighter/bomber was built. Affectionately known as the "Wooden Wonder", this famous aircraft played a conspicuous role during World War II. Salisbury Hall now houses a museum of de Havilland aircraft.
7. Where the track turns sharp left, go through a gate on to a road and turn left. Immediately turn right beside a white house to pass between buildings. Continue past the entrance to the Hall itself to the main approach road on the right.
8. Continue past the approach road to go on round a sharp left-hand

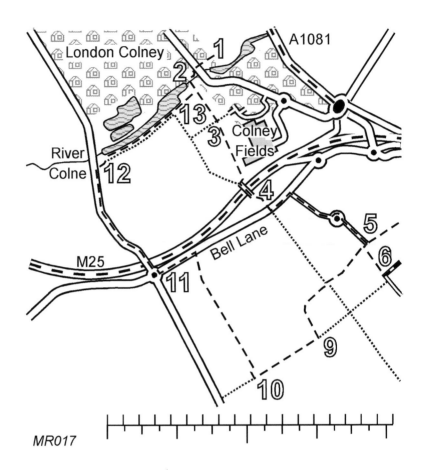

MR017

corner. Now go west towards farm buildings ahead. Where the concrete road veers away left, continue straight on along a wide gravel track, crossing your earlier route after 300 yd (Step 5). Keep along this track, crossing another path after 300 yd, and then go round a pronounced left-hand bend, reaching a T-junction after a quarter of a mile.

9. Turn right with a high hedge on the right and continue for a quarter mile to a gap in the hedge just after passing under power cables.

10. Turn right through the gap, right again into the neighbouring field

and then left along the edge of the field with the power cables overhead.

Continue for a third of a mile, past the entrance to a sports complex, to a grassy area with bushes and small trees and a high fence separating the area from Bell Lane. Keep to the right of a large power pylon to find a gate in the fence and gain access to the road. Turn left along the pavement to a roundabout.

11. Turn right to cross the road, carry on over the motorway and follow the road for a third of a mile to a signed footpath leading right, just

Salisbury
Hall
Museum

1800 yds
1 Mile

before a bridge over the River Colne.

12. Follow this path upstream, taking the left fork where it divides, to follow a route beside the river as it soon widens out like a lake. Continue along the river, going past a cross path where one way leads to a "ford" that may well be under deep water.

A few yards later, take the left fork as the path divides, and carry on beyond where the river narrows drastically, to a cross path with the footbridge and public house mentioned in Step 1 visible to the left.

13. Turn left and cross the footbridge, return past the public house and cross High Street to return to the start point.

18: Colney Street – Two More Rivers

This walk in the Colne Valley follows parts of the Ver-Colne Valley Walk. It starts from Drop Lane off Smug Oak Lane west of Colney Street, between Radlett and Park Street on the A5 south of St. Albans.

OS Explorer 182, Land Ranger 166,
Distance: 4.5 miles (7.1 km),
Time: 2½ hours,
No shorter route is available,
Park: Car park in Drop Lane 100 yd from Smug Oak Lane – AL2 3TZ, GR TL150021
Route: Estate and farm tracks, bridle-ways and quiet lanes, paths may be muddy or even flooded after rain or high water levels, several climb-over stiles and one notable hill, not suitable for dogs as horse pastures must be crossed,
Access: Abbey Line trains to Bricket Wood (walk down Drop Lane to start from point 11),
Buses No. 621 at Bricket Wood,
Buses No 655 and 656 at Colney Street on A5183 between St Albans and Radlett,
Refreshments: Several public houses near Bricket Wood Station and at Moor Mill near the start.

The St. Michael's Ramblers first walked this route on March 6, 2010.

1. Leave the car park from the north-east corner (i.e. opposite the car entry) to follow a footpath which runs north between the River Ver and Drop Lane to the bridge in Smug Oak Lane.
2. Cross the bridge and immediately turn right into a narrow lane leading uphill. There is a finger post indicating a footpath diagonally across the field on the right. However as no recent sign of this path has been noted, continue along the lane for 150 yd to a climb-over stile and farm track on the right.
3. Follow this track between fields for a third of a mile until it reaches the banks of the River Colne opposite a large house.
4. Turn right and follow the footpath along the edge of a field beside the river.
5. Where the field ends, cross a bridge over a drainage ditch and follow the path into some scrub-land. Continue along the path for a further 200 yd until a hard gravel estate track is reached. Turn left along this track to cross a bridge over the river and continue to the end where a tarmac track crosses it.
6. Turn right and walk along this track as it curves right with large buildings on the right and fields on the left. Carry on along the track, which soon changes to a bridle path that is almost straight. After half a mile the path kinks left to pass a pumping station beside the river.
7. Beyond the pumping station, the path has a right kink followed by a very much longer curve to the left. Continue along the path for a further half mile soon seeing water meadows on the right. Maps indicate that the field sloping up on the left is the site of a Roman villa. However, there is now nothing to be seen.

58

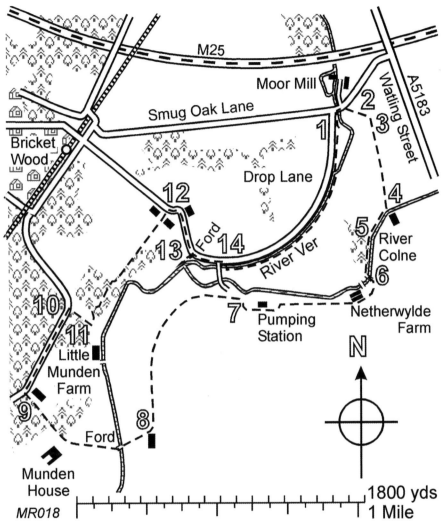

M25

Moor Mill

Smug Oak Lane

Watling Street

A5183

1

2

3

Bricket Wood

Drop Lane

12

4

Ford

13

14

River Ver

5

River Colne

6

10

7

Pumping Station

Netherwylde Farm

11

Little Munden Farm

N

9

8

Ford

Munden House

1800 yds
1 Mile

MR018

Soon after passing a wide trough and gate across the path to prevent the access of motor vehicles, there is a lane on the left, and a house on the right with a gate beside it.

8. Go through the gate and walk along a gravel track with a sign to a ford. **This track can be flooded after rain!** Cross the footbridge beside the ford and continue along the track up a slope.

Bear slightly right between buildings, passing a riding stable on the right. Continue up the slope with woods alternating on either side to a lane.

9. Turn right along the lane for a quarter mile. Just as the lane makes a sharp turn to the left, see an estate track on the right leading to Little Munden Farm.

10. Turn down the track for 150 yd to a gate stile on the left.

11. Go through this gate and follow the path over a narrow field, through another gate stile, and then climb up to woodland. Continue along the path through the woods and emerge in an open field that often accommodates horses. Keep straight on, eventually passing between houses to a lane.

12. Turn right and follow the lane down to a ford with stepping stones across the River Ver.

13. **Do not cross the river here as the water is deep, the current can be strong and the stepping stones are often submerged!** Turn right along a footpath beside the river and walk for 100 yd to view the confluence of the Rivers Ver and Colne. Then retrace your steps to the lane and continue on beside the river for about 200 yd to the start of a Waterside Walk.

14. Cross the river using the footbridge and follow the paved walk, complete with jokey wood carvings, two-thirds of a mile back to the car park.

19: Cholesbury Common – A Ridge Walk

This walk starts on Cholesbury Common, north of Chesham in Bucks. The route follows a ridge of the Chilterns south-east across farmland before returning along a shady path beside a wood in the valley bottom west of the ridge.

OS Explorer 181, Land Ranger 165,
Distance: 5.5 miles (8.9 km),
Time: 3 hours,
A 2.8 mile (4.4 km) version is shown,
Park: On grass verge beside Vale Road on Cholesbury Common – HP5 2UH, GR SP935070

Route: Field paths and country lanes, parts of the route are steep and it may be muddy after rain, many climb-over stiles,
Not suitable for dogs as there may be livestock in the fields and the stiles are without dog access,
Access: Bus No. 194 (Wednesday only) from Tring to Chesham,
Refreshments: Public house on Cholesbury Common.

The St. Michael's Ramblers first walked this ramble on May 28, 2011.

---

1. Walk south-east along a well-defined path that follows the left side of Vale Road. After 400 yd, cross a lane leading down to the left and continue a further 300 yd.
2. Cross Vale Road and enter a signed path into woods, with a row of houses to the left. Beyond the gardens, turn left to follow a path that jinks along behind the row of gardens. Just before the path turns sharp left at the end of the gardens, take a path that veers away half right.
3. Continue along this path across a small field, over a stile then through a gate into the corner of a farmyard. Go straight on along the path, which now has a hedge on the left, to climb a further stile. Cross a footpath and continue straight on towards a substantial house (Hawridge Place). The path is now quite obviously near the top of the ridge.
4. Follow the path as it goes to the left of Hawridge Place, over a series of stiles in a narrow alley, then crosses the main approach drive. Beyond gardens, climb more stiles, cross a narrow muddy lane and continue across an open field. Pass to the right of another large house (Hawridge Court).
5. For the shorter walk, turn right on a downhill path, at the bottom of the hill, turn right on a footpath beside a hedge and go on to Point 10. For the complete walk, continue along the upper path through a wide gap between hedges. This

path crosses open fields along the top of a broad ridge with distant views to the south.

6. After a mile, the path turns sharp left beside a hedge. Follow the path as it sweeps right to a junction of paths at the bottom left corner of the field.

7. Turn right at the bottom of the field along a hedge and after 200 yd turn left down a short flight of steps.
Continue first with a hedge then a fence on the right.
After admiring any livestock that may be on the other side of the fence, go over the stile in the corner of the field on to a wide track.

8. Turn right and then almost immediately enter a grassy path on the far side of the track. Follow this path as it turns left uphill towards a gate. Then just before the gate, turn right on another track along the edge of a wood and continue for 400 yd.

9. Where the track turns left to climb up into the woods, turn right down a short side path to a clearly visible stile in the edge of the wood. Climb over the stile and turn left along the path beside the wood. Follow this path for a mile, first beside woods, then beside a wide hedge to reach the narrow muddy lane described under Point 4.

10. Cross the lane and follow the path for a further three-quarters of a mile across open fields and twisting through a wood.
Finally, the path goes past some ruined farm buildings and a cottage before emerging on a short driveway. Walk straight along the drive to a lane.

62

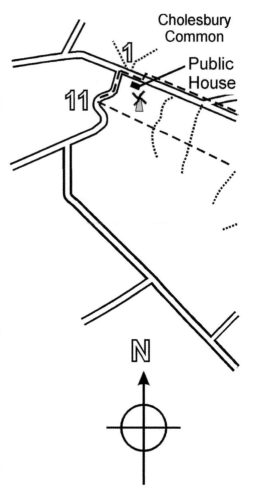

MR019

11. Turn left up the lane climbing steeply for 200 yd past houses and a windmill to return to the start point on Cholesbury Common.

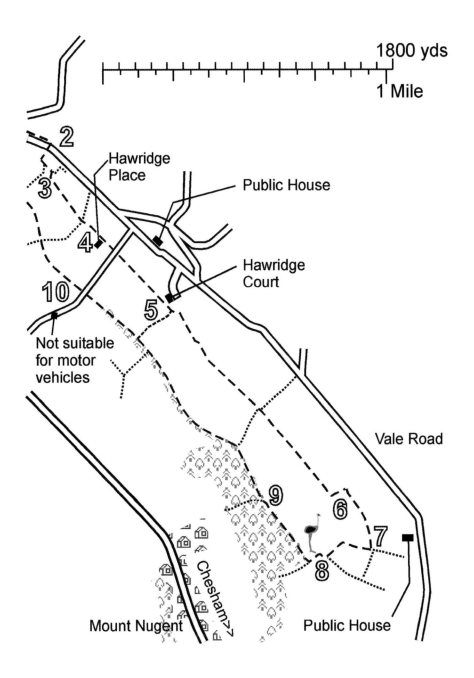

1800 yds

1 Mile

2

Hawridge
Place

3

Public House

4

10

Hawridge
Court

5

Not suitable
for motor
vehicles

Vale Road

9

6

7

8

Mount Nugent

Chesham⟩⟩

Public House

20: Jockey End – North to Studham

This walk starts from Jockey End at the northern end of Gaddesden Row and offers fine vistas of the gentle southern edge of the Chilterns on the way to Studham.

OS Explorer 174/194, Land Ranger 166
Distance: 6.4 miles (10.25 km),
Time: 3½ hours,
No shorter version is available,
Park: On road at Jockey End or parking bays in West Dene –
HP2 6HU, GR TL040138,
Route: Village pavements, estate and farm tracks, field and woodland paths. Some paths may be muddy after rain, no stiles, three noteworthy hills, not suitable for dogs as the route crosses playing fields,
Access: Buses, some X31 services between Dunstable and Hemel Hempstead via Jockey End and Studham,
Refreshments: Public houses at Studham.

The St. Michael's Ramblers first walked this route on June 1, 2013.

1. Start from the junction of Gaddesden Row and Bradden Lane and walk south-east along the pavement of Gaddesden Row, towards Redbourn.
2. Just beyond the last house on the left, turn left into a children's playground. Keep to the left edge of the playground and leave by a path running beside house gardens, which descends towards a row of trees.
3. Go through a gap in the trees and down some steps to a woodland

64

track (Dean Lane). Turn right along this track and walk down for half a mile until it reaches a lane.
4. Go through the gate stile in the lane just left of the end of the track to climb up across a field, aiming

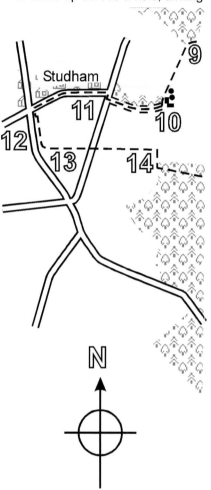

MR020

between two small but prominent trees with a row of poplars to their right.

5. Go through a gate stile under the trees and enter a school playing field. Turn right along the edge of the field to pass to the right of some cricket nets.

Follow the path behind the nets and walk under trees to emerge on the main drive into Beechwood Park School.

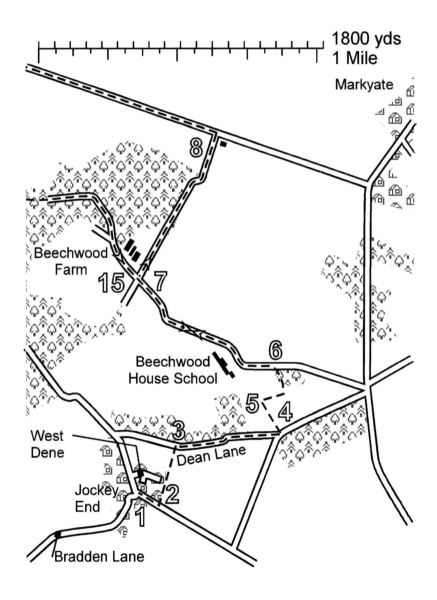

1800 yds
1 Mile

Markyate

Beechwood Farm

Beechwood House School

West Dene

Dean Lane

Jockey End

Bradden Lane

6. Join the drive and turn left to follow it uphill, continuing where it bears right past the front of the school. Keep on beyond the school where the drive becomes a gravel track that curves left past a modern cottage. Continue along the track for two-thirds of a mile past another house on the left to a cross track near Beechwood Farm.

7. Take the right-hand track and follow it for two-thirds of a mile down a gentle slope with woods to the left. Continue up a steeper section to reach the end of a tarmac road from the right beside a house.

8. Turn left to walk along a wide straight grassy track (Roe End Lane) for three-quarters of a mile.

9. Continue on this track round a sharp left turn with a very thick hedge on the right for a further quarter mile to a sewage works.

10. Turn right along a concrete drive and follow it for 400 yd to the Byslips Road.

11. **This road carries fast-moving traffic.**
Cross the road and enter Kenilworth Road opposite. Keep to the right as this road has no pavement.
Continue to a junction with the Dunstable Road opposite the war memorial on Studham Common. There is a public house opposite, beside the common, and another to the right further up Dunstable Road.

12. Just left of this junction is a lay-by with an "upside down" map of Studham Common and a gate leading to two footpaths. Take the path to the right and walk uphill beside the Dunstable Road to a T-junction with a cross path coming from the road.

13. Turn left and follow the path, high on the side of the hill to recross the Byslips Road.
This road carries fast-moving traffic.
From the crossing, continue on the same line for 400 yd past another "upside down" map to a T-junction with a cross path and a thick hedge beyond.

14. Turn right and walk up this path for 100 yd, and then go left to enter woods on a marked path that soon widens into a gravel track. Parts of this wood are a designated nature reserve. Continue along the track, crossing the end of a track coming up from the left. Go round a steady bend to the right, soon after which the track emerges from the wood to join a track from the right. Follow this track left, past Beechwood Farm.

15. At the crossroads just beyond the farm, carry straight on re-entering the track past Beechwood Park School. Go past the school to rejoin the main drive and continue to Point 6.
At Point 6, turn left by the sign to follow the footpath back through Dean Lane to the steps on the left (Point 3).
Turn left up the steps and follow the path back across the field to the children's play area (Point 2). Turn right along the pavement to return to the start point.

21: A Short Walk from Whipsnade Tree Cathedral

This short ramble starts from the Whipsnade Tree Cathedral at Whipsnade village, in the Chilterns west of Dunstable, and follows the top of the scarp slope, offering fine views of the Bedfordshire Plain.

OS Explorer 193/194, Land Ranger 165/166
Distance: 3 miles (4.8 km),
Time: 1¾ hours,
No shorter version is shown,
Park: In the Cathedral car park 300 yd east of LU6 2LF, GR TL009181 or in one of the other car parks shown,

These directions are given from the Tree Cathedral car park. To start from other car parks, follow directions from the relevant Point (4 or 6),
Route: Footpaths, quiet lanes and bridleways, no step-over stiles, two very short climbs, paths may be muddy after rain,
Access: Bus No. X31 from Luton,
Refreshments: Visitor Centre along the route.

The St. Michael's Ramblers first walked this route on September 13, 2005.

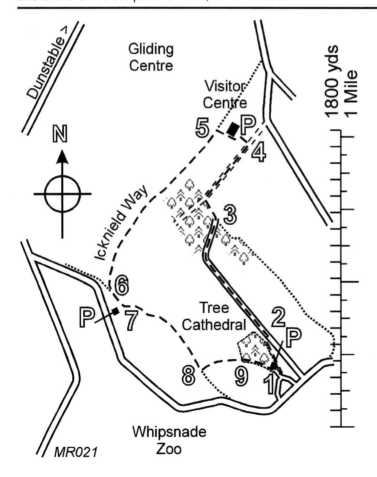

MR021

The Tree Cathedral was constructed as an act of faith after the First World War, and is laid out in the form of a medieval cathedral. Planting began in the nineteen-thirties.

1. Leave the Tree Cathedral car park, walk back to the lane and turn sharp left along a signed footpath that runs back beside the cathedral. Opposite a gate leaving the cathedral on the left, turn right along a short path to a tarmac lane.
2. Turn left along the lane and continue for half a mile going past a bend to the right then a sharper bend left to where the tarmac finishes and motor traffic is blocked by metal posts.
3. Go 100 yd beyond the posts, along the edge of a wood, and turn right on a straight tarmac track. Continue along this track for a quarter mile, passing under two sets of power lines, to a concrete path going to the Visitor Centre and car park.
4. Turn left past the Visitor Centre, down a slope to a tall metal structure (a wind catcher).
5. Turn left along the Icknield Way path. Carry on along the Way for more than half a mile, past several marker posts and through several gate stiles, until the route dips down towards a lane and Bison Hill car park.
6. Follow the Icknield Way marker posts up a slight gradient, round a tight bend to the left and enter a track between hedges, with a field on the right.
7. Continue along the track as it slowly turns right again, eventually passing to the right of a row of cottages.
8. Beyond the cottages, where there are two parallel tracks, turn left to follow a sign for the Tree Cathedral.
Climb gently past a donkey sanctuary as the path bears left towards the cathedral.
9. Go through a gate stile into the cathedral. Continue along the path which returns to the car park and start point.

22: Streatley to Sharpenhoe Clappers in the Chilterns

This walk starts high on the Chiltern Hills and crosses the beech-covered summit of Sharpenhoe Clappers a few miles north of Luton in Bedfordshire. This site is suggested as a possible original for Bunyan's Delectable Mountains. The route descends a long flight of steep steps (about 160) to reach the Bedfordshire plain, crossing farmland before climbing slowly back to the start point again.

OS Explorer 193, Land Ranger 166,
Distance: 5.2 miles (8.3 km),
Time: 3 hours,
A 3.0 mile (4.8 km) version is shown,

Park: National Trust car park Sharpenhoe Clappers –
GR TL065296, on the right, one mile north of Streatley (LU3 3PS) on the Sharpenhoe Road,
Route: Farm tracks, footpaths, pavements, very high and steep steps, several strenuous hills and climb-over stiles, paths and steps may be muddy after rain,
Access: Buses No. 79 to Streatley,
Refreshments: Public houses in Streatley and Sharpenhoe.

The St. Michael's Ramblers first walked this route on July 5, 2008.

---

1. Go through the gate by the National Trust sign and walk downhill eastwards on a tarmac track between trees. The track becomes a gravel path, climbing and starting to bear left with woods on one side and a field on the other.
2. Ignore other paths that leave to left and right and continue along the path with views to the northwest as it crosses the open hillside with bushes close by on the right. Where the path enters beech trees towards the top of the hill, there is a short steep chalky slope that is often slippery – make a detour to the right to come around this slope. Then continue along the line of the path towards a memorial column standing among the trees.
3. From the column, walk almost straight on along an obvious path between low bushes to pass close to the highest point of the hill.

Continue this line straight on to the edge of the beech trees where a path runs beside bushes at the top of a steep slope down.
Turn left along this path for a few yards to the top of a long series of steps down to the right. **These steps may be slippery.** Go down this staircase of about 160 steps to reach the bottom of the hill.
4. At the bottom of the steps, the path straight on goes to Sharpenhoe village. Turn sharp left beneath some power cables and continue down a path to a gate stile. Go through the stile and turn half left

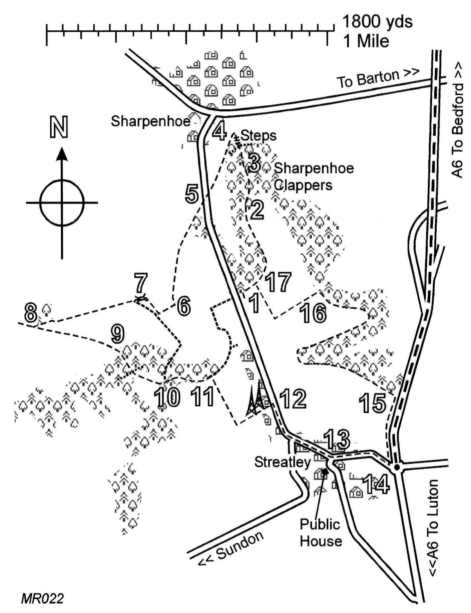

1800 yds
1 Mile

N

To Barton >>

A6 To Bedford >>

Sharpenhoe

4 Steps

3 Sharpenhoe Clappers

5

2

7

17

6

1

16

8

9

10 11

12

15

13

Streatley

14

Public House

<< Sundon

<<A6 To Luton

MR022

towards a house that can be seen at an angle across the field.

5. Leave the field by a gate almost opposite the house and cross the lane to enter a track that starts to the right of the house. Follow this track as it gradually bends left

along the edge of the field with a hill getting higher to the left.

6. After half a mile following the track, turn right along a fenced path that crosses the field towards a nearby row of trees. Turn right by the trees which have a small stream beside

them and follow the edge of the field to find the footbridge.

7. For the shorter 3-mile walk, cross the bridge, and turn left along the line of trees. Some way beyond the source of the stream, the path turns right to climb steeply into the wood above. **This climb**, which **can be very greasy**, rejoins the main route just beyond Point 10. For the complete walk, cross the bridge and walk straight on along the left edge of a field for half a mile until a small wood is encountered on the right.

8. Go through a gap in the field divider to the left and turn almost back to cross a field on a well-defined path that climbs a gentle slope.

9. At the far edge of the field, climb over a stile to follow the path up into a scrubby area. The path soon runs among larger trees and reaches another track close to the far side of the wood.
Cross this track to leave the wood almost straight ahead via a gate to follow a path that continues to climb across another field towards more woods.

10. Follow the path into the wood, passing the top of the path described in Point 7. Go on along the level path, continuing for some yards beyond where it starts running along the right side of the wood.

11. For the shorter walk keep straight on with a steep down slope to the left while the path curves left.

Ignore a path leading right, then when your path leaves the slope, turn sharp right on to a footpath back to the start point.
For the complete walk, turn right along a straight path with a high hedge on the left. After 400 yd, turn left and continue with the hedge on the left, beyond a pair of high antennae to reach the Streatley to Sharpenhoe road.

12. Turn right and follow pavements into Streatley and a public house. **Take care: roads around the village carry a surprising amount of heavy traffic.**

13. Turn down along the road towards the A6 Luton to Bedford road, continuing beyond houses and allotments, almost as far as the roundabout.

14. Turn left between the last allotment and the A6 to follow a path that climbs beside the main road towards trees.

15. Turn left along the edge of the trees and follow a wide path for a mile as it winds along the top of a steep wooded northern slope.

16. Go through a gap in the only hedge that crosses this path and turn left to walk on a fenced path along the edge of a field beside the hedge. About halfway along the hedge, turn right and walk between fences across the field.

17. At the far side of the field, turn left to rejoin the outward tarmac path and return to the start point at the car park.

23: Kimpton to Peters Green

This walk, a few miles north-east of Harpenden, describes a "Lazy Eight" across an open Chiltern landscape between Kimpton and Peters Green.

OS Explorer 182, Land Ranger 166,
Distance: 6.2 miles (9.9 km),
Time: 3¼ hours,
Two shorter routes are also shown:
1.8 miles (2.9 km) on the Kimpton loop and 4.4 miles (7.0 km) with the Peters Green loop,
Park: On roads near Kimpton Post Office at the west end of the village by the junction of High Street and Claggy

Road – SG4 8PZ, GR TL172183
For the longer loop, park at Peters Green – LU2 9QP, GR TL142190
Route: Quiet lanes, farm tracks, footpaths, bridleways, paths may be muddy after rain, no climb-over stiles,
Access: Buses No. 44, 45, 304 and 315 at Kimpton, 44 at Peters Green,
Refreshments: Public houses in Kimpton and Peters Green.

The St. Michael's Ramblers first walked this route, finishing in a thunderstorm, on August 25, 2012.

1. Start from Kimpton Post Office on the corner of High Street and Claggy Road. Walk along Claggy Road away from the junction. The pavement ends where the houses finish. Traffic visibility beyond the village is good as there are no roadside hedges. Carry on along this quiet road for half a mile between fields to a junction where the Luton Road comes down from the left.
2. **Beware as this road carries more traffic and there are now hedges.** Turn right along the Luton Road and after a few yards go past a turning on the right that runs down through the shallow depression of Claggybottom. Continue straight on where the Luton Road leaves to the right after 100 yd, and go a quarter mile to a sharp bend right, just before the junction surrounded by farms at Ansells End.
3. For the shorter Kimpton loop, turn left just before the apex of the bend and follow the grassy path downhill

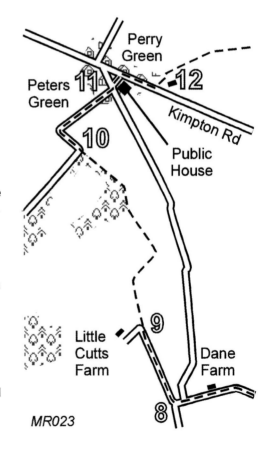

described from Point 15. For the complete walk, continue to the Ansells End junction, then turn left and follow another quiet lane for a third of a mile down to a junction with the Kimpton Road.

4. Cross the road, turn right then left into the driveway for Ramridge Farm.

5. Immediately after the drive turns right towards the farm buildings, turn left along a grassy path to the right of a house. Follow this path downhill for a quarter mile with a hedge on the right, then up across a field to a small wood.

6. Turn right just inside the wood and left again beyond it to continue a further quarter of a mile down a bridleway to a road.

7. **Beware: this narrow road carries a lot of traffic.** Turn right along the road, past Dane Farm and a first lane on the right.

8. Where the road bends sharp left, turn up a second lane on the right.

9. After 200 yd, where this lane turns sharp left, go straight on along a twisty bridleway that runs between hedges for three-quarters of a mile to emerge on a sharp bend in another lane.

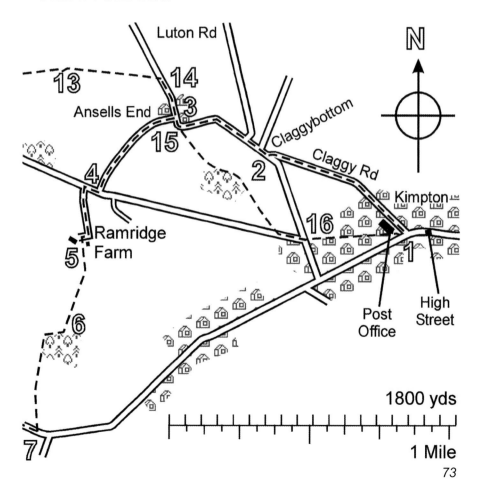

10. Turn right and follow the lane for 300 yd round a right-angle bend to the right, and on to the triangle in Peters Green village.
11. For the longer Peters Green loop, start from the triangle with the public house on your right and carry on with Points 12 to 15, then continue from Points 4–10.
For the complete route, walk straight on past the triangle and public house, cross Kimpton Road, turn right and go beyond the last house to a chapel.
12. Start along the footpath beside a hedge to the left of the chapel and soon goes through the hedge. Turn right and follow a wide grassy track across open fields for half a mile until the way ahead is blocked by a hedge.
13. Go through a large gap in the hedge to the right and turn left immediately to go through a gate stile almost hidden in the hedge. Then resume the same heading, but now on a footpath. Continue along this path for another third of a mile until it emerges through a gate stile on a lane.
14. Turn right and follow the lane up over a hill to reach the junction at Ansells End again.
15. For the longer loop, turn right at the junction and follow Points 4–10 back to Peters Green.
For the complete walk, go past the lane to the right. Just beyond the apex of the left bend, turn right and start along a grassy path that goes slowly downhill across open fields. Continue along this path as it curves round the side of a wood to the right and heads towards a sign-post at the far edge of the field ahead.
At the sign, where this path joins the Kimpton Road, turn left and, staying in the field, follow the edge of the field down to a T-junction with the Luton Road.
16. Cross the road and go through the stile opposite the Kimpton Road and keep straight ahead along a further footpath.
17. Continue for a quarter of a mile along the approach to Kimpton between high garden fences, then finally re-emerge beside the post office at the start point.

24: Lemsford to Sandridge

This walk from Lemsford north of Hatfield goes through ancient woodland where old-time charcoal burners worked.

OS Explorer 182, Land Ranger 166,
Distance: 7.3 miles (11.7 km),
Time: 4 hours,
A 4.5 mile (7.2 km) version is shown,
Park: Lay-by opposite the entry to Brocket Park near St. John's Church at Lemsford - AL8 7TT, GR TL215120

Route: Farm tracks, footpaths and some lane walking, several climb-over stiles, paths may be muddy after rain,
Access: Buses No. 365, 366 and 636 to Lemsford and No. 304 and 320 to Sandridge,
Refreshments: Public houses in Lemsford and Sandridge.

The St. Michael's Ramblers first walked this route on February 2, 2008.

1. **Beware: the B653 road carries fast-moving traffic.**
   From the lay-by, carefully cross the busy B653 Wheathamstead Road and turn left along the pavement. Follow this until opposite Cromer Hyde Lane a few yards beyond a public house.
2. Recross the B653 to walk up Cromer Hyde Lane.
3. Soon after the end of the first group of houses, where the woods finish on the right, enter the wide track on the left. Follow this track as it gradually bends right then more sharply to the left to pass the end of a hedge.
4. Turn right and follow a wide straight path between fields. This passes a small copse on the left, followed by a small pond (Dogsheart Spring).
5. Continue on this path, passing left of Symonshyde Farm to a lane with the extensive Symondshyde Great Wood on the opposite side. Much of the woodland in this area was the haunt of charcoal burners up until the 1930s and early1940s. Turn right along the lane for a few yards, and then turn left through a

gate into the wood. Follow the tarmac path through the trees to reach a T-junction at the further side of the wood.
6. For the shorter walk, turn right and follow the footpath north just inside the edge of the wood, to Hammond's Lane between Hammond's Farm and Tower Hill Lane.
   Then turn right and continue from Step 11.
   For the complete walk, turn left and follow the path south inside the edge of the wood. After half a mile, the path emerges from the wood and follows a hedge on its left. Continue along this path to gates on to a lane by Fairfolds Farm.
7. Turn right and follow the lane (Woodcock Hill) west. There may be some traffic along this lane, but the mostly low banks on either side should allow approaching vehicles to be seen in good time.
   Continue along the lane past a radio station and descend towards Sandridge.
8. At the edge of the village where the lane turns sharp left, enter the

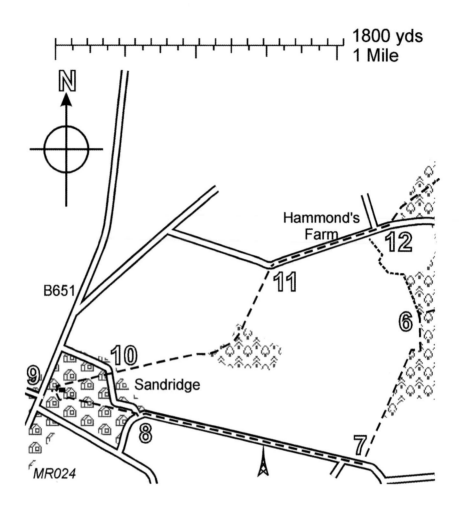

footpath on the left corner of Langley Green. Go along the path between gardens to Church End that leads into Sandridge High Street where there are both public houses and shops.

9. Enter the churchyard and follow a path to the left of the church which leaves by the furthest corner. Continue behind gardens to reach Langley Green again.

10. Cross Langley Green and go between the houses to continue along a path running uphill across open fields towards a small wood. Continue along the path through a corner of the wood to Hammond's Lane.

11. Turn right and follow the lane to a stile in the fence on the left, 100 yd beyond Tower Hill Lane and just before the garden of a large house.

12. Climb over the stile and follow the path north-east between fences. The path soon runs beside a wood, gradually bearing left. It crosses a field, runs beside a smaller wood, and then to the right of a hedge

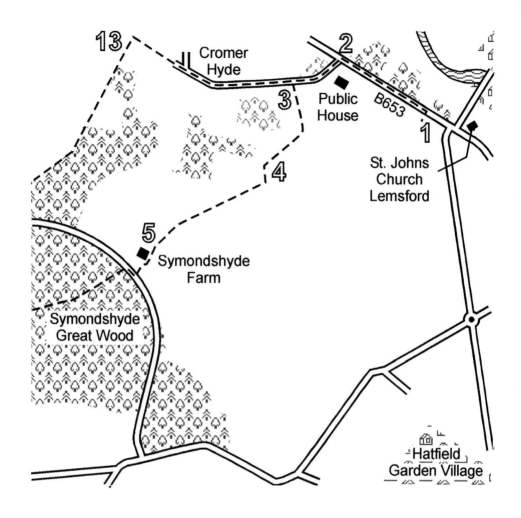

along another field to a T-junction with a cross path (the continuation of Cromer Hyde Lane).

13. Turn right and follow this path for half a mile to rejoin the outward route and return along Cromer

Hyde Lane. Carefully recross the Wheathampstead Road (B653) and turn right to follow it back to the start point.

25: Codicote to Mardley Hill

This walk starts by St. Giles Church, Codicote and runs east across fields via Rableyheath and Mardley Heath to Mardley Hill. It returns via Potters Heath.

OS Explorer 182, Land Ranger 166,
Distance: 5.5 miles (8.9 km),
Time: 3 hours,
A 3.6 mile (5.8 km) version is also shown,
Park: At the sports field opposite St. Giles Church in Bury Lane, Codicote – SG4 8XT, GR TL218187 or in the church car park,
Route: Footpaths, sections on quiet lanes and pavements, paths may be muddy after rain, several steep hills, and climb-over stiles, not suitable for dogs as the route crosses several fields that can contain livestock,
Access: Buses No. 44, 45, 314, 315, to Codicote, 300, 301 to Mardley Hill,
Refreshments: Public houses and cafes in Codicote and Mardley Hill.

The St. Michael's Ramblers first walked this route on February 5, 2011.

1. Start on Bury Lane opposite St. Giles Church. With the church on your left, walk down the pavement for 80 yd and cross the lane and enter a signed footpath along a drive.
   Take the centre path where the way forks into three, and continue downhill between hedges. Pass through two gate stiles going straight on beyond the hedges.
2. At a junction of several paths, continue straight ahead for half a mile on a path climbing steeply then bearing left across fields to

Sally Deards Lane by Plummer's Farm.
3. Turn right along the lane, round a bend left, and take a signed footpath to the left where the lane starts to bend right again. Continue across a field for a further quarter mile to Slip Lane at Rableyheath.

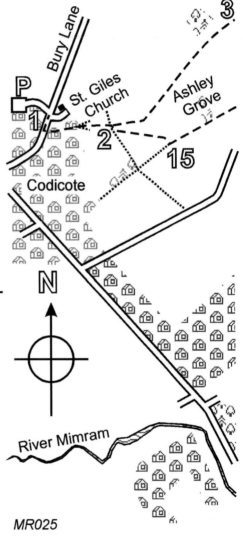

MR025

4. Turn right along the lane, then after 100 yd turn left into a signed path between the houses. At the end of the gardens, turn right on a path behind them and 100 yd beyond the gardens, bear right around a small pond to meet another path. Turn left along this path and continue on the left side of a field to reach Spinney Lane where it joins Wych Elm Lane end to end.

5. Turn right along Spinney Lane **which can get busy with motor traffic.**
Then continue 200 yd to Ninnings Lane on the left.

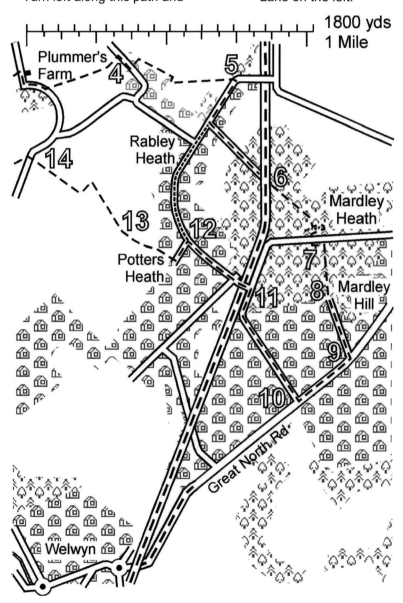

1800 yds
1 Mile

Plummer's Farm

Rabley Heath

Mardley Heath

Potters Heath

Mardley Hill

Great North Rd.

Welwyn

For the shorter walk, go past Ninnings Lane, continue on along Spinney Lane for half a mile as it bears left. Turn right into a farm drive and then continue from Point 12.

For the complete walk, turn left down Ninnings Lane, continuing straight on along Normans Lane. Motorway traffic will be heard and possibly also seen ahead. Go on past several farms and through a tunnel under the A1(M) motorway **that is also used by horses.**

6. On emerging, follow the path between fences and where these finish, go straight on uphill between trees into Mardley Heath. Follow the path as it bears right at the top of the hill and then left through a horse gate. Go right and left again, ignoring a path from the right, to a cross path beside a deep dip, with a flight of steps opposite. Go straight across to continue on a twisting path to the bottom of the steps. Climb the steps, and immediately turn right and follow the path beside a massive wooden barrier to reach Heath Road.

7. Cross Heath Road and turn left to follow a path beside another massive wooden barrier. Where the barrier turns away, continue following the path beside it. Where the barrier ends, bear slightly left to follow the marker posts on a steep downhill route through woodland in a southward direction.

8. Leave via an exit by a signboard to go down a path that becomes a gravel road (Hangman's Lane) and continue on to the Great North Road at Mardley Hill.

9. Turn right on the pavement, down past a public house and shops. As

this is approximately halfway through the walk, it may be a good place to consider refreshment.

10. Beyond the shops, turn right to climb the steep pavement of Cannonsfield Road. Where the houses end at the top of the hill, the road bends right just before a junction to the left.

11. Turn left at the junction, go over the A1(M), then along Pottersheath Road, **which can become busy with motor traffic.**

12. Soon after the road bears right, turn left on a signed path along a farm drive. Just past the last house on the right, turn right along a path crossing a field.
Climb a step stile and continue in the same direction across a field with a hedge on the left to a hidden double step stile in the far left corner.

13. Climb only the first part of the stile, then continue straight across a field to a stile by a power pole that can be seen near the centre of the far fence. Climb this stile and follow a path between fences sharp left then sharp right to reach Rabley Heath Road after a quarter mile.

14. Cross the road to take the signed footpath almost opposite that runs diagonally left across an open field. Follow this path for half a mile, passing Ashley Grove on the right after a quarter mile.

15. Halfway between Ashley Grove and a small clump of trees ahead, turn right down a steep path towards St. Giles Church. Where several paths meet (Point 2) turn left uphill to return along the outward route to Bury Lane and the start point.